The Word for All Seasons

David Graham is Rector of Hayes, Kent
and is Secretary of the Liturgical Committee
of the Diocese of Rochester.

THE WORD FOR ALL SEASONS

Services of the Word for every Sunday of the Year and major Holy Days

David Graham

Illustrated by
Val and Charlie Edmondson

CANTERBURY PRESS

Norwich

First published in 2002 by the Canterbury Press Norwich
St Mary's Works, St Mary's Plain,
Norwich, Norfolk, NR3 3BH

Text © in this compilation David Graham 2002

Illustrations © Val and Charlie Edmondson 2002

British Library Cataloguing in Publication data
A catalogue record for this book is available
from the British Library

Bible readings are from the New Revised Standard Version of the Bible, Anglicized Edition, © 1989, 1995, the Division of Christian Education of the National Council of the Churches of Christ in the USA

The author is grateful to the following copyright-holders for permission to use their copyright texts:

The Common Worship authorised texts used for the Collect for Purity, the Penitential section, the Collects, and the Creeds are all copyright © The Archbishops' Council of the Church of England.
The following Affirmations of Faith are copyright texts:

'Christ died for our sins...' **Words: Michael Perry © Mrs B Perry / Jubilate Hymns**
USED BY PERMISSION

'We believe in God...' **Words: Michael Perry © Mrs B Perry / Jubilate Hymns**
USED BY PERMISSION

'Though he was divine...' **Words: Michael Perry © Mrs B Perry / Jubilate Hymns**
USED BY PERMISSION

Printed in Great Britain by Biddles Ltd
www.biddles.co.uk

This book is dedicated
to
the people of Saint Luke's Church
Bromley Common

CONTENTS

Preface	
The First Sunday of Advent	2
The Second Sunday of Advent	4
The Third Sunday of Advent	6
The Fourth Sunday of Advent	8
Christmas Day	10
The First Sunday of Christmas	12
The Second Sunday of Christmas	14
The Epiphany	16
The Baptism of Christ	18
The First Sunday of Epiphany	
The Second Sunday of Epiphany	20
The Third Sunday of Epiphany	22
The Fourth Sunday of Epiphany	24
The Presentation of Christ in the Temple	26
The Fifth Sunday before Lent	28
The Fourth Sunday before Lent	30
The Third Sunday before Lent	32
The Second Sunday before Lent	34
The Sunday Next before Lent	36
The First Sunday of Lent	38
The Second Sunday of Lent	40
The Third Sunday of Lent	42
Mothering Sunday	44
The Fourth Sunday of Lent	
The Fifth Sunday of Lent	46
Palm Sunday	48
Good Friday	50
Easter Day	52
The Second Sunday of Easter	54
The Third Sunday of Easter	56
The Fourth Sunday of Easter	58
The Fifth Sunday of Easter	60
The Sixth Sunday of Easter	62

The Seventh Sunday of Easter	64
Day of Pentecost	66
Trinity Sunday	68
The First Sunday after Trinity	70
The Second Sunday after Trinity	72
The Third Sunday after Trinity	74
The Fourth Sunday after Trinity	76
The Fifth Sunday after Trinity	78
The Sixth Sunday after Trinity	80
The Seventh Sunday after Trinity	82
The Eighth Sunday after Trinity	84
The Ninth Sunday after Trinity	86
The Tenth Sunday after Trinity	88
The Eleventh Sunday after Trinity	90
The Twelfth Sunday after Trinity	92
The Thirteenth Sunday after Trinity	94
The Fourteenth Sunday after Trinity	96
The Fifteenth Sunday after Trinity	98
The Sixteenth Sunday after Trinity	100
The Seventeenth Sunday after Trinity	102
The Eighteenth Sunday after Trinity	104
The Nineteenth Sunday after Trinity	106
The Twentieth Sunday after Trinity	108
The Twenty-First Sunday after Trinity	110
The Last Sunday after Trinity	112
Bible Sunday	
All Saints' Sunday	114
The Fourth Sunday before Advent	116
The Third Sunday before Advent	118
The Second Sunday before Advent	120
Christ the King	122
The Sunday Next before Advent	
The Transfiguration of our Lord	124
Harvest Festival	126
A Saint's Day	128

PREFACE

This collection of liturgies for every Sunday of the Church Year is offered to clergy, readers and other worship leaders of the Church of England as an easy-to-use, flexible resource for non-eucharistic worship in a wide variety of situations, such as

- all-age worship
- services for every season
- youth services
- informal worship in prisons, universities, hospitals or residential homes
- A Liturgy of the Word service that leads into the Liturgy of the Sacrament

To meet these requirements the liturgies have the following features

- a clear Anglican shape and content, with a freshness of touch and a potential for congregational participation, young and old, throughout
- a wide use of Biblical material that builds on the premise that this is a 'Service of the Word', helping the congregation to become familiar with the Scriptural foundations that underlie our beliefs and worship
- a strong seasonal element that gives worshippers a greater awareness of the church calendar and enriches their worship as they engage with the unfolding story of salvation

All the liturgies follow the structure of 'A Service of the Word', and use authorised texts for the Penitential section, Collect and Affirmation of Faith, as laid down in Common Worship. Biblical material is from the New Revised Standard Version. Some of the opening prayers and intercessions are from Common Worship; most are original.

The liturgies have been developed and used over a period of six years at St. Luke's Church, Bromley Common. I am grateful to the congregation for their patient and active participation in a process of on-going liturgical formation. The liturgies are now offered to the wider church in the hope that they will be of use to hard-pressed clergy, readers and worship leaders for the enrichment of public worship in many different settings. They may be freely quarried as resource material for use in other services, photocopied as complete orders of service, or this publication may itself be used as a congregational service book. The enclosed disk contains the whole text in *Word* format.

SOME NOTES ABOUT THE LITURGIES

THE SEASONAL INTRODUCTION

Each liturgy is prefaced by a brief introduction about the festival or season in which it is being used. This is designed to help the congregation begin to engage with the church's worship on that Sunday by reminding and informing them of the significance of the occasion. It also makes them more aware of the church calendar and thereby more engaged with the story of salvation as it unfolds through the church year. The liturgies cover every Sunday including those major festivals that occasionally fall on a Sunday such as Christmas Day, The Epiphany, The Presentation of Christ in the Temple, The Transfiguration of our Lord and All Saints' Day. There are also liturgies for Mothering Sunday, Good Friday, Harvest Festival and A Saint's Day.

Where there is no particular season or festival to mark – such as during 'Ordinary Time' – a brief exposition of the Collect of the Day is offered for meditation before worship begins, although this is not intended to be a theme for the whole service.

THE GATHERING

This opening section of the liturgy is entitled 'The Gathering', following Order One Common Worship rather than 'The Preparation' as in 'A Service of the Word', because it seems a more appropriate description of this part of the service. It also serves to remind people of a common structure that underlies both eucharistic and non-eucharistic worship.

The Greeting

After the formal greeting by the service leader to the whole congregation, the next section could be led by a lay person, young or old. This is usually a responsive scriptural passage, relevant to the season when possible, that enables the congregation to praise God, or think about his purposes, in biblical language. Occasionally, non-biblical responses are used, with suggestions for visual aids or symbolic actions.

The Greeting section is brought to a close with a prayer, sometimes the Collect for Purity – expressing another link with the eucharist – or an alternative prayer that also prays for God's help in our worship of him. Optional provision is then made for a time of informal singing of worship songs. Other presentations or activities may also take place. Starred marks indicate that, at this point in many churches, the children leave for their own group sessions.

Penitence

The Penitential section often begins with a biblical quotation leading into a time of quiet reflection. This is followed by an authorised general confession (from Order One) and an authorised absolution (from Order One, or from 'A Service of the Word'). On many Sundays a worked-out confession, based on the 'Kyrie' format, is used instead of, or in addition to, the general confession. The purpose is to encourage worshippers to make their confession in a thoughtful way.

After the Absolution, optional provision is made for the singing or saying of the Gloria (particularly appropriate if the Liturgy of the Sacrament is to follow), or Venite, Song or Responses. The text of the Gloria can be found on page xiii.

Collect of the Day

'The Gathering' section culminates in the Collect of the Day which is printed out so that all may participate fully in the offering of this prayer.

THE LITURGY OF THE WORD

Scripture Readings

The pattern in this section follows Order One, with the same congregational responses to the reading of the scriptures. Provision is also made for the Gospel to be preceded by a gradual psalm, hymn or scriptural song.

Affirmation of Faith

The Nicene Creed is printed out for the major festivals. On other Sundays authorised Affirmations of Faith, that may relate to the current season, are provided. The text of the Nicene Creed can be found on page xiv.

THE PRAYERS

Intercessions

The Prayers are devised in a way that allows intercessors, clergy or lay, to contribute special thanksgivings, prayers or intentions, either prayed altogether at the beginning, or interposed in the responsive general intercession that follows, at the places indicated. The aim of this format is to give freedom to intercessors to create prayers relevant for their local church context but within an overall framework that helps to stimulate ideas for prayer, and ensures important elements of public prayers (such as prayers for the state and the bishop) are usually included.

The Lord's Prayer

The Lord's Prayer would normally be omitted here if the Liturgy of the Sacrament followed. Its text, in both traditional and contemporary forms, appears on page xiii.

The Concluding Prayer

The Concluding Prayer takes varied forms: a biblically-based prayer, a familiar collect from Common Worship, a 'classic' prayer by a saint of the church, or a Celtic prayer of benediction. The Service finishes with the Blessing or the Grace.

ACKNOWLEDGEMENTS

I would like to thank the many people who have contributed to the evolution of this book: those who have commented on the material and the people of Saint Luke's Church, Bromley Common with whom it has been tested over the past six years. I would particularly like to express my gratitude to Beverley Kane and Marie Nasso who have typed the manuscripts and patiently incorporated the many amendments. I am also grateful to my wife and children for their forbearance and encouragement as this book has gradually come to fruition.

GLORIA IN EXCELSIS

Glory to God in the highest,
and peace to his people on earth.
Lord God, heavenly King, almighty God and Father,
we worship you, we give you thanks,
we praise you for your glory.
Lord Jesus Christ, only Son of the Father,
Lord God, Lamb of God,
you take away the sin of the world:
have mercy on us;
you are seated at the right hand of the Father:
receive our prayer.
For you alone are the Holy One,
you alone are the Lord,
you alone are the Most High, Jesus Christ,
with the Holy Spirit,
in the glory of God the Father. Amen.

THE LORD'S PRAYER

Contemporary	*Traditional*
Our Father in heaven,	Our Father, who art in heaven,
hallowed be your name,	hallowed be thy name;
your kingdom come,	thy kingdom come;
your will be done,	thy will be done;
on earth as in heaven.	on earth as it is in heaven.
Give us today our daily bread.	Give us this day our daily bread.
Forgive us our sins	And forgive us our trespasses,
as we forgive those who sin against us.	as we forgive those who trespass against us.
Lead us not into temptation	And lead us not into temptation;
but deliver us from evil.	but deliver us from evil.
For the kingdom, the power,	For thine is the kingdom,
and the glory are yours	the power and the glory,
now and for ever.	for ever and ever.
Amen.	Amen.

THE NICENE CREED

We believe in one God, the Father, the Almighty,
maker of heaven and earth, of all that is, seen and unseen.
We believe in one Lord, Jesus Christ,
the only Son of God,
eternally begotten of the Father,
God from God, Light from Light,
true God from true God,
begotten, not made, of one being with the Father;
through him all things were made.
For us and for our salvation he came down from heaven,
was incarnate from the Holy Spirit and the Virgin Mary
and was made man.
For our sake he was crucified under Pontius Pilate;
he suffered death and was buried.
On the third day he rose again
in accordance with the Scriptures;
He ascended into heaven
and is seated at the right hand of the Father.
He will come again in glory to judge the living and the dead,
and his kingdom will have no end.
We believe in the Holy Spirit, the Lord, the giver of life,
who proceeds from the Father and the Son,
who with the Father and the Son is worshipped and glorified,
who has spoken through the prophets.
We believe in one holy catholic and apostolic Church.
We acknowledge one baptism for the forgiveness of sins.
We look for the resurrection of the dead,
and the life of the world to come. Amen.

The Word for All Seasons

THE FIRST SUNDAY OF ADVENT
'Put on the armour of light'

A new Church Year begins today. The four weeks of Advent (Latin *adventus* – coming) are about the coming of God's Kingdom. It is a season of hope in which we look forward to 'the last day when Christ shall come again' to establish that Kingdom on earth. We also look back to those who have figured in the unfolding story of God's coming to rule his people in justice and peace.

The Gathering

THE GREETING
May the light and love of Christ be with you.
And also with you.

(A HYMN may be sung)

LIGHTING OF THE ADVENT CANDLE
(Children may gather round the Advent Wreath)

The candles in our Advent Wreath will remind us of the story of how, through the years, through different people, and finally in Jesus Christ, God's Kingdom comes on earth.

Advent 1 – Patriarchs and Leaders
Blessed be God who called Abraham and Sarah, Isaac and Jacob, Moses and David to be the founders and leaders of his people Israel. **Blessed be God for ever.**

Abraham and Sarah were promised that, through their descendants, all the world would be blessed. **Thanks be to God.**

Moses and David, good and faithful leaders of God's people, paved the way for a greater One to follow. **Thanks be to God.**

(The first candle is lit)

As we light this first candle we celebrate the faith of Abraham and Sarah, Isaac and Jacob, Moses and David.
**Like them we put our faith in God
who fulfilled his promises
by sending his Son Jesus Christ
to be the Saviour and King of all. Amen.**

(SONGS may be sung)

* * * * *

PENITENCE
God calls human beings to account for the stewardship of their lives …

Lord, we confess we have not always used our time and our gifts wisely, creatively and unselfishly:
forgive us for misusing or wasting them.
Lord, have mercy.

Lord, we have not always lived in your light, or reflected it into the world's darkness:
forgive us for being set in our ways or complacent.
Christ, have mercy.

Lord, we have sometimes ended the day in anger or hurt: forgive us for being unrepentant or unforgiving.
Lord, have mercy.

The almighty and merciful Lord
grant *us* pardon and forgiveness of all *our* sins, time for amendment of life,
and the grace and strength of the Holy Spirit.
Amen.

(The VENITE, a SONG or RESPONSES may be used)

THE COLLECT OF THE DAY
Let us pray …   *(silent prayer)*

Almighty God, give us grace to cast away the works of darkness and to put on the armour of light, now in the time of this mortal life, in which your Son Jesus Christ came to us in great humility; that on the last day, when he shall come again in his glorious majesty to judge the living and the dead, we may rise to the life immortal;
through him who is alive and reigns with you, in the unity of the Holy Spirit, one God, now and for ever.   **Amen.**

The Liturgy of the Word

THE SCRIPTURE READING(S)

(After the reading)
This is the Word of the Lord.
Thanks be to God.

PSALM/HYMN or SCRIPTURAL SONG

THE GOSPEL

Hear the Gospel of our Lord Jesus Christ according to N.
Glory to you, O Lord.

(After the reading)
This is the Gospel of the Lord.
Praise to you, O Christ.

THE SERMON

AFFIRMATION OF FAITH

Let us affirm our faith in God:

***I believe in God, the Father almighty,
creator of heaven and earth.
I believe in Jesus Christ,
his only Son, our Lord, who was
conceived by the Holy Spirit,
born of the Virgin Mary,
suffered under Pontius Pilate,
was crucified, died, and was buried;
he descended to the dead.
On the third day he rose again;
he ascended into heaven,
he is seated at the right hand of the
Father, and he will come
to judge the living and the dead.
I believe in the Holy Spirit,
the holy catholic Church,
the communion of saints,
the forgiveness of sins,
the resurrection of the body,
and the life everlasting.   Amen.***

(The Apostles' Creed)

(A HYMN may be sung)

The Prayers

INTERCESSIONS

(Special thanksgivings and prayers ...)

*('Maranatha' – from the Aramaic language spoken by Jesus – means 'Our Lord, come.'
Used in Christian worship from early times.)*

God, our Father in heaven, we pray that when your Son Jesus Christ comes again as King and Judge, he will find us neither dead in sin nor asleep in apathy but alive in the Spirit and obedient in his service. Help us this Advent, and always, to prepare for his coming.
Maranatha.   **Come, Lord Jesus.**

Father God, we long for that Day when every person will acknowledge Jesus as their Saviour and King. Give your Spirit to your people that we may be witnesses of Christ's saving grace and agents of his peace.
Maranatha.   **Come, Lord Jesus.**

Father God, we long for that Day when the prejudice and fears that divide people will lose their power, and all wrongs will be put right. We pray for our Queen and the leaders of this and every nation …
Strengthen us to break down barriers, work for justice, and heal the world's brokenness.
Maranatha.   **Come, Lord Jesus.**

Father God, we long for that Day when there will be no more sorrow or pain. We pray for those who suffer now from grinding poverty, aching loneliness, or prolonged ill-health …
Bless those who care for them, and grant to all who are in need, healing and strength, perseverance and hope.
Maranatha.   **Come, Lord Jesus.**

Father God, we remember with thanksgiving those who have died …
Grant us with them, and with all the saints …
a share in your eternal kingdom,
through Jesus Christ our Lord.   **Amen.**

THE LORD'S PRAYER

(A HYMN may be sung)

CONCLUDING PRAYER

May the God of peace himself
sanctify you entirely:
and may your spirit and soul and body be kept sound and blameless at the coming of our Lord Jesus Christ.   **Amen.**

(1 Thess. 5:23)

(THE BLESSING or THE GRACE is said)

THE SECOND SUNDAY OF ADVENT
'Lord, raise up your power and come among us'

> The four weeks of Advent are a season of hope: we pray and prepare for the day when God's Kingdom will come among us with 'power ... and great might' (as today's Collect puts it). The first Advent Candle represents the **Patriarchs** and first leaders of Israel through whom God's rule on earth dawned. Today we remember the **Prophets** of Israel who challenged Israel to return to God's ways.

The Gathering

THE GREETING
May the light and love of Christ be with you.
And also with you.

(A HYMN may be sung)

LIGHTING OF THE ADVENT CANDLES
(Children may gather round the Advent Wreath)

The candles in our Advent Wreath remind us of the story of how, through the years, through different people, and finally in Jesus Christ, God's Kingdom comes on earth.

The first candle reminds us of the Patriarchs and first leaders of God's people: Abraham and Sarah, Isaac and Jacob, Moses and David.

Advent 2 - The Prophets
Today is the Second Sunday of Advent: we remember the Prophets, and how God spoke through them to challenge evil, injustice and unbelief among the people.
Arise, shine, for your light has come.

Isaiah said, 'A child is born to us! A Son is given to us! He will be called Wonderful Counsellor, Mighty God, Eternal Father, Prince of Peace.'
Arise, shine, for your light has come.

(The second candle is lit)

As we light this candle we remember Isaiah, Jeremiah, Micah and all the prophets who had unshakeable hope in the purposes of God.
Like them we put our faith in God who fulfilled his promises by sending his Son Jesus Christ to be the Saviour and King of all. **Amen.**

(SONGS may be sung)
* * * * *

PENITENCE
God calls human beings to account for the stewardship of their lives ...

Lord, we confess we have not always used our time and our gifts wisely, creatively and unselfishly: forgive us for misusing or wasting them.
Lord, have mercy.

Lord, we have not always lived in your light, or reflected it into the world's darkness: forgive us for being set in our ways or complacent.
Christ, have mercy.

Lord, we have sometimes ended the day in anger or hurt: forgive us for being unrepentant or unforgiving.
Lord, have mercy.

The almighty and merciful Lord
grant *us* pardon and forgiveness of all *our* sins, time for amendment of life,
and the grace and strength of the Holy Spirit.
Amen.

(The VENITE, a SONG or RESPONSES may be used)

THE COLLECT OF THE DAY
Let us pray ... *(silent prayer)*

O Lord, raise up, we pray,
your power and come among us, and with great might succour us; that whereas, through our sins and wickedness we are grievously hindered in running the race that is set before us, your bountiful grace and mercy may speedily help and deliver us; through Jesus Christ your Son our Lord, to whom with you and the Holy Spirit, be honour and glory, now and for ever. **Amen.**

The Liturgy of the Word

THE SCRIPTURE READING(S)
(After the reading)
This is the Word of the Lord.
Thanks be to God.

PSALM/HYMN or SCRIPTURAL SONG

THE GOSPEL
Hear the Gospel of our Lord Jesus Christ according to N.
Glory to you, O Lord.
(After the reading)
This is the Gospel of the Lord.
Praise to you, O Christ.

THE SERMON

AFFIRMATION OF FAITH
Let us affirm our faith in God:
**I believe in God, the Father almighty, creator of heaven and earth.
I believe in Jesus Christ, his only Son, our Lord, who was conceived by the Holy Spirit, born of the Virgin Mary, suffered under Pontius Pilate, was crucified, died, and was buried; he descended to the dead. On the third day he rose again; he ascended into heaven, he is seated at the right hand of the Father, and he will come to judge the living and the dead.
I believe in the Holy Spirit, the holy catholic Church, the communion of saints, the forgiveness of sins, the resurrection of the body, and the life everlasting. Amen.**
(The Apostles' Creed)

(A HYMN may be sung)

The Prayers

INTERCESSIONS
(Special thanksgivings and prayers ...)
('Maranatha' – from the Aramaic language spoken by Jesus – means 'Our Lord, come.' Used in Christian worship from early times.)

Our Father in heaven, we bring you our prayers for the Church and for all people. Send your Holy Spirit to equip them with the gifts that are needed to serve you:

For our bishop N. and all ministers of God's word and sacraments, that they may serve your Church in love, and build up your people in truth and faith ...
Maranatha. **Come, Lord Jesus.**

For the peace and well-being of the world, for our Queen and the leaders of the nations and for the resolution of deep and bitter conflicts ...
Maranatha. **Come, Lord Jesus.**

For the innocent victims of violence or injustice, and for all who strive to overcome evil with good ...
Maranatha. **Come, Lord Jesus.**

For our families and those close to us, and for all who need our time, our attention and our care ...
Maranatha. **Come, Lord Jesus.**

We give thanks for our community, for all who serve us, and those who cherish us ... Strengthen the bonds of trust and respect within families, communities and workplaces ...
Maranatha. **Come, Lord Jesus.**

For the sick, the suffering, the sorrowful and the dying, and for all who bring healing and hope to them ...
Maranatha. **Come, Lord Jesus.**

We remember with thanksgiving those who have died ...
Father of all **grant us with them, and all the saints, a share in your eternal Kingdom, through Jesus Christ our Lord. Amen.**

THE LORD'S PRAYER
(A HYMN may be sung)

CONCLUDING PRAYER
May the God of peace himself sanctify you entirely: and may your spirit and soul and body be kept sound and blameless at the coming of our Lord Jesus Christ. **Amen.**
(1 Thess. 5:23)

(THE BLESSING or THE GRACE is said)

THE THIRD SUNDAY OF ADVENT
John the Baptist: 'sent to prepare Christ's way'

We have passed the half-way stage in the Advent Season, during which we hope, pray and prepare for the coming of God's Kingdom. From now on our attention is increasingly focused on Jesus Christ whose birth at Bethlehem was the sign that God's rule was near. Today we remember John the Baptist who was sent to prepare the way for Christ, by 'turning the hearts of the disobedient'.

The Gathering

THE GREETING
May the light and love of Christ be with you.
And also with you.

(A HYMN may be sung)

LIGHTING OF THE ADVENT CANDLES
(Children may gather round the Advent Wreath)

The candles in our Advent Wreath remind us of the story of how, through the years, through different people, and finally in Jesus Christ, God's Kingdom comes on earth.

The first candle reminds us of the Patriarchs and first leaders of Israel.
The second candle reminds us of the Prophets who urged the people to return to God's ways and to look forward to a future King who would bring peace to the world.

Advent 3 – John the Baptist
Today, the Third Sunday of Advent, we remember John the Baptist who was sent to prepare the way for the Lord. John said, 'Repent, for the Kingdom of heaven has come near.'
Blessed be the Lord the God of Israel.

John saw Jesus and exclaimed,
'Look! the Lamb of God
who takes away the sin of the world!'
Blessed be the Lord the God of Israel, for he has come to his people and set them free.

(The third candle is lit)

We light this third candle for John and his shining witness to the Christ.
Go before the Lord to prepare his way.
(from the Benedictus C.W.)

(SONGS may be sung)

* * * * *

PENITENCE
John exposed the complacency and corruption of his day, and called people to repent. Let us confess our sins to the Lord:

When our deeds do not match our fine words,
Lord, have mercy. **Lord, have mercy.**

When we let evil go unchallenged, and are afraid to speak the truth,
Christ, have mercy. **Christ, have mercy.**

When we are preoccupied with ourselves, and give little attention to others,
Lord, have mercy. **Lord, have mercy.**

When we trust in earthly treasures more than in God's unfailing care,
Christ, have mercy. **Christ, have mercy.**

The almighty and merciful Lord
grant *us* pardon and forgiveness of all *our* sins, time for amendment of life,
and the grace and strength of the Holy Spirit.
Amen.

(The VENITE, a SONG or RESPONSES may be used)

THE COLLECT OF THE DAY
Let us pray … *(silent prayer)*

O Lord Jesus Christ, who at your first coming sent your messenger to prepare your way before you: grant that the ministers and stewards of your mysteries may likewise so prepare and make ready your way by turning the hearts of the disobedient to the wisdom of the just, that at your second coming to judge the world we may be found an acceptable people in your sight; for you are alive and reign with the Father in the unity of the Holy Spirit, one God, now and for ever.
Amen.

The Liturgy of the Word

THE SCRIPTURE READING(S)

(After the reading)
This is the Word of the Lord.
Thanks be to God.

PSALM/HYMN or SCRIPTURAL SONG

THE GOSPEL
Hear the Gospel of our Lord Jesus Christ according to N.
Glory to you, O Lord.

(After the reading)
This is the Gospel of the Lord.
Praise to you, O Christ.

THE SERMON

AFFIRMATION OF FAITH
Let us proclaim our faith in God:

Do you believe and trust in God the Father, source of all being and life, the one for whom we exist?
We believe and trust in him.

Do you believe and trust in God the Son who took our human nature, died for us, and rose again?
We believe and trust in him.

Do you believe and trust in God the Holy Spirit, who gives life to the people of God and makes Christ known in the world?
We believe and trust in him.

This is the faith of the Church.
This is our faith.
We believe and trust in one God,
Father, Son and Holy Spirit. **Amen.**

(A HYMN may be sung)

The Prayers

INTERCESSIONS
(Special thanksgivings and prayers …)

John the Baptist prepared people for the coming of Jesus by the washing away of their sins. Lord, grant that, during this Advent season, we may prepare to celebrate Christ's coming, not with greed and excess but in penitence and simplicity.
Your Kingdom come, **your will be done.**

John challenged people from all walks of life to repent and change their ways. Lord, we pray for bishop N. and all church ministers. Send the Holy Spirit to inspire them as they teach, challenge and build people up in the Christian life.
Your Kingdom come, **your will be done.**

John pointed people to Jesus, never to himself. We pray for those who, in a media-driven culture, receive fame and fortune ... Save us from striving to be the centre of attention; give us humility and integrity, whatever life may bring.
Your Kingdom come, **your will be done.**

John spoke boldly against injustice, immorality and greed. We pray for our country, our Queen and the leaders of the nations …
Give them the strength to resist corruption and promote justice, peace and community.
Your Kingdom come, **your will be done.**

John knew the isolation and humiliation of prison. Be close, Lord, to all who suffer today from rejection, loneliness or ill-health … Grant them strength and healing, patience and encouragement.
Your Kingdom come, **your will be done.**

We remember with thanksgiving those who have died … Grant us with them, with John and all the saints, the hope of your eternal Kingdom, through Jesus Christ our Lord.
Amen.

THE LORD'S PRAYER

(A HYMN may be sung)

CONCLUDING PRAYER
May the God of hope fill us
with all joy and peace in believing,
by the power of the Holy Spirit. **Amen.**
(Rom. 15:13)

(THE BLESSING or THE GRACE is said)

THE FOURTH SUNDAY OF ADVENT
The Virgin Mary 'looked for Christ's coming'

We have celebrated the Advent season in hope, anticipating the day when Christ will come again to establish God's Kingdom of justice and peace everywhere. We have also looked back to the Patriarchs, the Prophets, and to John the Baptist who, in different ways, were servants of God's rule in Israel. Today we remember the Virgin Mary, the mother of Jesus. In him God's rule on earth was finally realized.

The Gathering

THE GREETING
May the light and peace of Christ be with you.
And also with you.

(A HYMN may be sung)

LIGHTING OF ADVENT CANDLES
(Children may gather round the Advent Wreath)

The candles in our Advent Wreath recall the story of how, through the years, through different people, and finally in Jesus Christ, God's Kingdom comes on earth.

The first candle reminds us of the Patriarchs and leaders of Israel. The second candle reminds us of the Prophets of Israel. They all looked forward to the coming of a King who would bring justice and peace. The third candle reminds us of John the Baptist, sent to prepare the way for Jesus.
Bless the Lord, you servants of the Lord.

Advent 4 – The Virgin Mary
Today is the Fourth Sunday of Advent when we remember the Virgin Mary. The angel said to her:
'Do not be afraid, Mary, for you have found favour with God ... You will bear a son and will name him Jesus ... He will be called Son of God.' Mary said:
'Here am I, the servant of the Lord:
let it be with me according to your word.'
                                    (Luke 1:30ff.)
(The fourth candle is lit)

As we light this fourth candle,
we give thanks for Mary
who was obedient to God's call and, like her, we rejoice in Christ's coming among us:
My soul proclaims the greatness of the Lord, my spirit rejoices in God my Saviour.

(from the Magnificat, Common Worship)

(SONGS may be sung)
                    * * * * *

PENITENCE
The Virgin Mary gave herself fully to doing God's will.
Let us confess our failings in the service of our Lord.
When we are faced with a challenge, but regress into old attitudes,
Lord, have mercy.   *Lord, have mercy.*
When we face difficult times but fail to trust in your good purposes,
Christ, have mercy.   *Christ, have mercy.*
When we look inwards to our selfish concerns rather than outwards to a world in need,
Lord, have mercy.   *Lord, have mercy.*
When we are agents of gloom rather than messengers of hope,
Christ, have mercy.   *Christ, have mercy.*

The almighty and merciful Lord
grant *us* pardon and forgiveness of all *our* sins, time for amendment of life,
and the grace and strength of the Holy Spirit.

(The VENITE, a SONG or RESPONSES may be used)

THE COLLECT OF THE DAY
Let us pray ...   *(silent prayer)*

God our Redeemer,
who prepared the Blessed Virgin Mary to be the mother of your Son: grant that, as she looked for his coming as our Saviour, so we may be ready to greet him when he comes again as our Judge; who is alive and reigns with you, in the unity of the Holy Spirit,
one God, now and for ever.   *Amen.*

The Liturgy of the Word

THE SCRIPTURE READING(S)

(After the reading)
This is the Word of the Lord.
Thanks be to God.

PSALM/HYMN or SCRIPTURAL SONG

THE GOSPEL

Hear the Gospel of our Lord Jesus Christ according to N.
Glory to you, O Lord.

(After the reading)
This is the Gospel of the Lord.
Praise to you, O Christ.

THE SERMON

AFFIRMATION OF FAITH

Let us affirm our faith in God:

**I believe in God, the Father almighty, creator of heaven and earth.
I believe in Jesus Christ, his only Son, our Lord, who was conceived by the Holy Spirit, born of the Virgin Mary, suffered under Pontius Pilate, was crucified, died, and was buried; he descended to the dead. On the third day he rose again; he ascended into heaven, he is seated at the right hand of the Father, and he will come to judge the living and the dead.

I believe in the Holy Spirit, the holy catholic Church, the communion of saints, the forgiveness of sins, the resurrection of the body, and the life everlasting. Amen.**

(The Apostles' Creed)

(A HYMN may be sung)

The Prayers

INTERCESSIONS

(Special thanksgivings and prayers ...)

An intercession based on the Magnificat:

Mary said: 'The Almighty has done great things for me.'
We thank you, Father God, for all the good things you have done for us ... Save us from ever taking your blessings for granted.
Lord, hear us.   **Lord, help us.**

'He has mercy on those who fear him.'
Father, trusting in your mercy,
we pray for our Church and diocese:
for bishop N. and all who serve the Church:
Fill your people with the Holy Spirit that we may bear witness to Christ in the home, the workplace and the neighbourhood.
Lord, hear us.   **Lord, help us.**

'He has scattered the proud ... casting down the mighty.'
Father, we pray for all who hold high positions: our Queen, and the leaders of the nations ...
Give them wisdom, humility and honesty in their service of the people, that peace, justice and true fellowship may abound.
Lord, hear us.   **Lord, help us.**

'He has filled the hungry with good things.'
Father, we pray for all who lack food or water, shelter or work, and all who are ill or in pain ...
Strengthen the hands of those who care, and grant to suffering people the wholeness they long for.
Lord, hear us.   **Lord, help us.**

We remember with thanksgiving those who have died ...
Grant us with them, with Mary and all the saints, the hope of your eternal Kingdom, through Jesus Christ our Lord.   **Amen.**

THE LORD'S PRAYER

(A HYMN may be sung)

CONCLUDING PRAYER

Father God, help us to accept, like Mary, the challenge to serve you, whether the task you give is great or small. May our lives bring glory to Christ, our Saviour and King. **Amen.**

(THE BLESSING or THE GRACE is said)

CHRISTMAS DAY
'To you is born ... a Saviour'

Today the Church celebrates the astonishing fact that the almighty, infinite God took on the risk and frailty of human life, and Jesus was born of the Virgin Mary. The purpose of his life was, as the angels sang, to bring God's peace and goodwill to all people on earth. Through Jesus, therefore, the long-awaited Kingdom of God was finally to be realized.

The Gathering

THE GREETING
I bring you good news of great joy for all the people; to you is born this day in the city of David a Saviour
who is the Messiah, the Lord.   *(Luke 2:10)*

(A CAROL may be sung)

For the birth of Jesus your Son, our Saviour, cradled in a manger at Bethlehem,
we thank you, heavenly Father.

For the love and gentle care of Mary, his mother, most blessed of all women,
we thank you, heavenly Father.

For shepherds keeping watch over their flocks by night, who came with haste to worship Christ, the new-born King,
we thank you, heavenly Father.

For the goodwill of this Christmas season, in our hearts and in our homes, bringing joy and gladness to us all,
we thank you, heavenly Father.

And in our joyful gratitude we join our voices with the angels who are always singing to you,
Holy, holy, holy Lord,
God of power and might,
heaven and earth are full of your glory;
Hosanna in the highest.   **Amen.**

(SONGS may be sung)

* * * * *

PENITENCE
Hear the words of the angel to Joseph:
'You shall call his name Jesus
for he will save his people from their sins.'
Therefore let us seek forgiveness from God through Jesus the Saviour of the world:

Jesus, Emmanuel, God-with-us,
forgive our unwelcoming hearts ...
Lord, have mercy.   **Lord, have mercy.**

Jesus, Son of God, Servant of humanity,
forgive our self-centred lives ...
Christ, have mercy.   **Christ, have mercy.**

Jesus, Prince of Peace, Hope of the nations,
forgive our bitter conflicts ...
Lord, have mercy.   **Lord, have mercy.**

Jesus, Saviour of the world,
Friend of sinners,
forgive our self-righteous attitudes ...
Christ, have mercy.   **Christ, have mercy.**

May Almighty God, who sent his Son into the world to save sinners, bring *us* his pardon and peace, now and for ever.   **Amen.**

(THE GLORIA may be sung)

THE COLLECT OF THE DAY
Let us pray ...   *(silent prayer)*

Almighty God,
you have given us your only-begotten Son to take our nature upon him and at this time to be born of a pure virgin:
grant that we, who have been born again and made your children by adoption and grace, may daily be renewed
by your Holy Spirit;
through Jesus Christ your Son our Lord,
who is alive and reigns with you,
in the unity of the Holy Spirit,
one God, now and for ever.   **Amen.**

The Liturgy of the Word

THE SCRIPTURE READING(S)

(After the reading)
This is the Word of the Lord.
Thanks be to God.

PSALM or CAROL

THE GOSPEL
Hear the Gospel of our Lord Jesus Christ according to N.
Glory to you, O Lord.

(After the reading)
This is the Gospel of the Lord.
Praise to you, O Christ.

THE SERMON

AFFIRMATION OF FAITH
We believe in one God, the Father, the Almighty, maker of heaven and earth, of all that is, seen and unseen.

We believe in one Lord, Jesus Christ, the only Son of God, eternally begotten of the Father, God from God, Light from Light, true God from true God, begotten, not made, of one Being with the Father; through him all things were made.

For us and for our salvation he came down from heaven, was incarnate from the Holy Spirit and the Virgin Mary, and was made man.
For our sake he was crucified under Pontius Pilate; he suffered death and was buried.
On the third day he rose again in accordance with the Scriptures; he ascended into heaven and is seated at the right hand of the Father.
He will come again in glory to judge the living and the dead, and his Kingdom will have no end.

We believe in the Holy Spirit, the Lord, the giver of life, who proceeds from the Father and the Son, who with the Father and the Son is worshipped and glorified, who has spoken through the prophets.

We believe in one holy catholic and apostolic Church. We acknowledge one baptism for the forgiveness of sins.
We look for the resurrection of the dead, and the life of the world to come. Amen.
(The Nicene Creed)

(A CAROL may be sung)

The Prayers

INTERCESSIONS
(Special thanksgivings and prayers …)

Jesus, born of Mary, hear our prayers for mothers who are caring for their babies …
In your mercy, **Lord Jesus, come near.**

Jesus, laid in a manger, hear our prayers for children who have no safe home, no loving family or no proper nourishment …
In your mercy, **Lord Jesus, come near.**

Jesus, saved from Herod's brutal deeds, hear our prayers for all who live in fear and danger …
In your mercy, **Lord Jesus, come near.**

Jesus, brought up to think of others first, hear our prayers for the young today, growing up in a culture of greed and excess …
In your mercy, **Lord Jesus, come near.**

Jesus, destined to die for the sins of the world, hear our prayers for all who have not yet received your forgiveness.
In your mercy, **Lord Jesus, come near.**

Jesus, welcomed into this world by angels and shepherds, help us to celebrate your birthday in joyful simplicity … **Amen.**

THE LORD'S PRAYER

(A CAROL may be sung)

CONCLUDING PRAYER
Loving God, may the Christmas morning make us happy to be your children and the Christmas evening bring us to our beds with grateful thoughts, forgiving and forgiven, for Jesus' sake.
Amen. *(R. L. Stevenson)*

(THE BLESSING or THE GRACE is said)

THE FIRST SUNDAY OF CHRISTMAS
'He shared in our humanity, so we may share in his divinity'

During the twelve days of the Christmas festival, the Church continues to celebrate the 'Incarnation' (Latin *incarnare* - to become flesh). This means God, in the birth of his Son Jesus Christ, became inextricably involved with human beings. He 'shared in our humanity', as today's Collect puts it, so that we, through Christ's saving work, 'may share the life of his divinity', and enjoy fellowship with God for ever.

The Gathering

THE GREETING
May the light and peace of Jesus Christ our Lord be with you.
The Lord bless you.

(A HYMN/CAROL may be sung)

Beloved, let us love one another,
because love is from God.

God's love was revealed among us in this way: God sent his only Son into the world
so that we might live through him.

In this is love, not that we loved God
but that he loved us

and sent his Son to be the atoning sacrifice for our sins.   *(1 John 4:7, 9-10)*

PRAYER
Father God, we give thanks for Christmas:

for the cards that keep us in touch with each other,   **we give thanks;**
for the gifts given and received with love,   **we give thanks;**
for the meals shared with family and friends,   **we give thanks;**
for good will and good cheer in dark times,   **we give thanks;**
for the story of Jesus' birth, re-told in words and music,   **we give thanks;**
for your gift to the world of its King and Saviour, Jesus Christ,
we give thanks and rejoice.   Amen.

(SONGS may be sung)

* * * * *

PENITENCE
Hear the words of the angel to Joseph:

'You shall call his name Jesus
for he will save his people from their sins.'
Therefore let us seek forgiveness from God through Jesus the Saviour of the world:

Jesus, Emmanuel, God-with-us,
forgive our unwelcoming hearts …
Lord, have mercy.   **Lord, have mercy.**

Jesus, Son of God, Servant of humanity,
forgive our self-centred lives …
Christ, have mercy.   **Christ, have mercy.**

Jesus, Prince of Peace, Hope of the nations,
forgive our bitter conflicts …
Lord, have mercy.   **Lord, have mercy.**

Jesus, Saviour of the world,
Friend of sinners,
forgive our self-righteous attitudes …
Christ, have mercy.   **Christ, have mercy.**

May Almighty God, who sent his Son into the world to save sinners, bring us his pardon and peace, now and for ever.   **Amen.**

(THE GLORIA, the VENITE, a SONG or RESPONSES may be used)

THE COLLECT OF THE DAY
Let us pray …   *(silent prayer)*
Almighty God,
Who wonderfully created us in your own image and yet more wonderfully restored us through your Son Jesus Christ:
Grant that, as he came to share in our humanity, so we may share
the life of his divinity;
who is alive and reigns with you,
in the unity of the Holy Spirit,
one God, now and for ever.   **Amen.**

The Liturgy of the Word

THE SCRIPTURE READING(S)

(After the reading)
This is the Word of the Lord.
Thanks be to God.

PSALM, HYMN/CAROL or SCRIPTURAL SONG

THE GOSPEL
Hear the Gospel of our Lord Jesus Christ according to N.
Glory to you, O Lord.

(After the reading)
This is the Gospel of the Lord.
Praise to you, O Christ.

THE SERMON

AFFIRMATION OF FAITH
Let us affirm our faith in Jesus Christ, the Son of God:

Though he was divine,
he did not cling to equality with God,
but made himself nothing.
Taking the form of a slave,
he was born in human likeness.
He humbled himself,
and was obedient to death –
even the death of the cross.
Therefore God has raised him on high,
and given him the name above every name:
that at the name of Jesus
every knee should bow,
and every voice proclaim
that Jesus Christ is Lord,
to the glory of God the Father. **Amen.**
(Phil. 2:6-11)

(A HYMN may be sung)

The Prayers

INTERCESSIONS
(Special thanksgivings and prayers ...)

Lord Jesus, born in the reign of Caesar Augustus, guide our Queen, the government, and the leaders of the nations;
may their decisions promote peace and justice in the world.

Lord Jesus, cradled in a squalid shed, be close to all who are homeless or in need,
and keep their hopes alive.

Lord Jesus, surrounded by the love of Mary and Joseph, bless all children born at this time,
and deepen the love between husbands and wives, parents and children.

Lord Jesus, visited by shepherds from nearby fields, prosper the work of our hands,
and direct the thoughts of our minds.

Lord Jesus, at risk from Herod's brutal power, defend the innocent from the bullies of this world,
and make us hospitable to refugees.

Lord Jesus, the Saviour, bring us out of darkness into your Light,
and fill us with your Spirit.

Lord Jesus, worshipped by wise men from afar, we offer our lives and gifts to you
that we may truly serve you in the world.

We remember with thanksgiving those who have died ... Grant us with them and with Joseph, Mary and the shepherds a share in your eternal Kingdom. **Amen.**

THE LORD'S PRAYER

(A HYMN/CAROL may be sung)

CONCLUDING PRAYER
Jesus, Son of God,
the news of your birth was proclaimed by the angels, and heard by the shepherds;
inspire the worship of your Church
and make us bearers of the good news
that God is with us always. **Amen.**

(THE BLESSING or THE GRACE is said)

THE SECOND SUNDAY OF CHRISTMAS
'Walk in his light and dwell in his love'

During the twelve days of the Christmas festival, the Church celebrates the 'Incarnation': the Son of God became a human being – Jesus Christ, 'one of us'. The light (or 'truth') of God and the love (or 'grace') of God flowed into the world through him. Today's Collect prays that we may learn to walk in that light and dwell in that love, which leads to the fullness of joy.

The Gathering

THE GREETING
May the light and peace of Jesus Christ our Lord be with you.
The Lord bless you.

(A HYMN/CAROL may be sung)

This is the message we have heard from him and proclaim to you,
that God is light and in him there is no darkness at all.

If we say that we have fellowship with him while we are walking in darkness,
we lie and do not do what is true;

but if we walk in the light
as he himself is in the light,
**we have fellowship with one another,
and the blood of Jesus Christ, his Son,
cleanses us from all sin.**

(1 John 1:5-7)

PRAYER
**Almighty God, to whom
all hearts are open, all desires known,
and from whom no secrets are hidden:
cleanse the thoughts of our hearts
by the inspiration of your Holy Spirit,
that we may perfectly love you,
and worthily magnify your holy name;
through Christ our Lord.   Amen.**

(SONGS may be sung)
* * * * *

PENITENCE
Christ the Light of the world has come to dispel the darkness of our hearts.
In his light let us examine ourselves and confess our sins …

The angel said to Joseph:
'You are to name him Jesus
for he will save his people from their sins.'
Therefore let us seek forgiveness from God through Jesus the Saviour of the world:

Jesus, Emmanuel, God-with-us,
forgive our ungrateful hearts …
Lord, have mercy.   **Lord, have mercy.**

Jesus, Son of God, Servant of humanity,
forgive our self-centred lives …
Christ, have mercy.   **Christ, have mercy.**

Jesus, Prince of Peace, Hope of the nations,
forgive our bitter conflicts …
Lord, have mercy.   **Lord, have mercy.**

Jesus, Saviour of the world, Friend of sinners,
forgive our self-righteous attitudes…
Christ, have mercy.   **Christ, have mercy.**

May Almighty God, who sent his Son into the world to save sinners, bring us his pardon and peace, now and for ever.   **Amen.**

(THE GLORIA, the VENITE, a SONG or RESPONSES may be used)

THE COLLECT OF THE DAY
Let us pray …   *(silent prayer)*

Almighty God, in the birth of your Son
you have poured on us the new light of your incarnate Word, and shown us the fullness of your love:
Help us to walk in his light and dwell in his love that we may know the fullness of his joy;
who is alive and reigns with you,
in the unity of the Holy Spirit,
one God, now and for ever.   **Amen.**

The Liturgy of the Word

THE SCRIPTURE READING(S)

(After the reading)
This is the Word of the Lord.
Thanks be to God.

PSALM, HYMN/CAROL or SCRIPTURAL SONG

THE GOSPEL
Hear the Gospel of our Lord Jesus Christ according to N.
Glory to you, O Lord.

(After the reading)
This is the Gospel of the Lord.
Praise to you, O Christ.

THE SERMON

AFFIRMATION OF FAITH
Let us affirm our faith in Jesus Christ, the Son of God:

Though he was divine,
he did not cling to equality with God,
but made himself nothing.
Taking the form of a slave,
he was born in human likeness.
He humbled himself,
and was obedient to death –
even the death of the cross.
Therefore God has raised him on high,
and given him the name above every name:
that at the name of Jesus
every knee should bow,
and every voice proclaim
that Jesus Christ is Lord,
to the glory of God the Father. **Amen.**
(Phil. 2:6-11)

(A HYMN/CAROL may be sung)

The Prayers

INTERCESSIONS
(Special thanksgivings and prayers ...)

Isaiah the prophet wrote:
Unto us a child is born, unto us a Son is given, and his name shall be called:
Wonderful Counsellor, Mighty God, Everlasting Father, Prince of Peace. *(9:6)*

Wonderful Counsellor,
give wisdom to governments and the leaders of the nations ...
Lord, hear us, **Lord, graciously hear us.**

Mighty God,
make the whole world know that you are King, and that all accountable to you ...
Lord, hear us, **Lord, graciously hear us.**

Everlasting Father,
bring all people to know your love for them.
Lord, hear us, **Lord, graciously hear us.**

Prince of Peace,
bring reconciliation wherever relationships have broken down, in families, communities and between nations ...
Lord, hear us, **Lord, graciously hear us.**

Son of God, Jesus Christ, you were born into the human family. You shared our weakness and suffering to reveal your Father's love:
draw near to those for whom Christmas brings little joy: the hungry, the homeless, the lonely, the sorrowful, the sick, and all who suffer ...
Bring to them, through us
and through all people of compassion,
your strength, light and hope.
for your mercy's sake. **Amen.**

THE LORD'S PRAYER

(A HYMN/CAROL may be sung)

CONCLUDING PRAYER
Jesus, Son of God,
the news of your birth was proclaimed by the angels, and heard by the shepherds;
inspire the worship of your Church
and make us bearers of good news,
that God is with us always. **Amen.**

(THE BLESSING or THE GRACE is said)

THE EPIPHANY
'Jesus - revealed as God's Son to the peoples of the earth'

The 'Epiphany' (Greek *epiphaneia* – revealing, manifesting) is celebrated on 6 January, the last day of the Christmas season. It refers to the revealing of Christ to the 'Magi', the Wise Men from the East who searched for truth and found it at Bethlehem. The main theme of the Epiphany season is the revelation of Christ as the light of the world and the King of all nations – Gentiles and Jews.

The Gathering

THE GREETING
The Lord of glory be with you.
The Lord bless you.

(A HYMN may be sung)

THE CHRIST IS REVEALED TO THE MAGI
A star leads the Wise Men to the manger.

Arise, shine; for your light has come
**and the glory of the Lord
has risen upon you.**
Nations shall come to your light
and Kings to the brightness of your dawn.
They shall bring gold and frankincense
and shall proclaim the praise of the Lord.
(Isa. 60:1, 3, 6)

(Symbols of the Wise Men's gifts may be presented)

What gifts are fitting for Christ our Lord?

Bring gold for the King of the nations
who rules us in justice and peace.

Bring frankincense for the Son of God
who reveals the Father's love.

Bring myrrh for the Son of Man
**who shared our sorrows and died for our sins.
Blessed be God for ever.**

PRAYER
Almighty God,
**to whom all hearts are open,
all desires known,
and from whom no secrets are hidden:
cleanse the thoughts of our hearts
by the inspiration of your Holy Spirit,
that we may perfectly love you,
and worthily magnify your holy name;
through Christ our Lord.   Amen.**

(SONGS may be sung)
* * * * *

PENITENCE
The story of the Wise Men challenges us about our commitment to God:

When we have grown tired of searching for truth or seeking God's will,
Lord, have mercy.

When we have strayed from the command to love and serve our neighbour,
Christ, have mercy.

When we have offered less than the best in our worship and service of God,
Lord, have mercy.

May almighty God
who sent his Son into the world to save sinners,
bring *us* his pardon and peace,
now and for ever.   **Amen.**

(The GLORIA, the VENITE, a SONG or RESPONSES may be used)

THE COLLECT OF THE DAY
Let us pray …   *(silent prayer)*

O God, who by the leading of a star manifested your only Son to the peoples of the earth: mercifully grant that we, who know you now by faith,
may at last behold your glory face to face;
through Jesus Christ your Son our Lord,
who is alive and reigns with you,
in the unity of the Holy Spirit,
one God, now and for ever.   **Amen.**

The Liturgy of the Word

THE SCRIPTURE READING(S)

(After the reading)
This is the Word of the Lord.
Thanks be to God.

PSALM/HYMN or SCRIPTURAL SONG

THE GOSPEL

Hear the Gospel of our Lord Jesus Christ according to N.
Glory to you, O Lord.

(After the reading)
This is the Gospel of the Lord.
Praise to you, O Christ.

THE SERMON

AFFIRMATION OF FAITH

At your Baptism you turned to Christ, repented of your sins, and renounced evil.

Do you now, at the start of a New Year, renew your allegiance to Christ?
We do, and with God's grace we will follow him as our Saviour and Lord.

Do you believe and trust in God the Father, source of all being and life, the one for whom we exist?
We believe and trust in him.

Do you believe and trust in God the Son, who took our human nature, died for us and rose again?
We believe and trust in him.

Do you believe and trust in God the Holy Spirit, who gives life to the people of God and makes Christ known in the world?
We believe and trust in him.

This is the faith of the Church.
This is our faith.
We believe and trust in one God, Father, Son and Holy Spirit. Amen.

(A HYMN may be sung)

The Prayers

INTERCESSIONS

(Special thanksgivings and prayers …)

The Wise Men offered gold to Christ, the King of all. Father, we pray for all who take authority to serve their country: our Queen, and the government of this and every nation … Give wisdom and integrity to all who lead, that their service will promote justice, peace and human well-being.
Your Kingdom come, **your will be done.**

The Wise Men offered frankincense to Christ, the Son of God. Father, we pray for the Church's life of worship and prayer, and for all who lead, teach and minister among us … Send the Holy Spirit to bless your servants with the gifts they need to build up the Body of Christ, and to strengthen us to be his witnesses in daily life.
Your Kingdom come, **your will be done.**

The Wise Men offered myrrh to Christ, the Son of Man. We pray for all who suffer from the injustices and frailties of human life … Bring deliverance to those who are trapped in grinding poverty, terrifying conflict or brutal oppression … Strengthen your servants who go to help them. Be close to all who suffer from pain or ill-health … Grant healing and hope to them all.
Your Kingdom come, **your will be done.**

We remember with thanksgiving those who have died … Grant us with them, and with Mary, Joseph and the Wise Men, a share in your eternal Kingdom, through Jesus Christ our Lord. **Amen.**

THE LORD'S PRAYER

(A HYMN may be sung)

CONCLUDING PRAYER

Christ our Lord, to whom kings bowed down in worship and offered gifts, reveal your glory to us, pour down the riches of your grace, and strengthen us to serve you in all the world. **Amen.**

(THE BLESSING or THE GRACE is said)

THE BAPTISM OF CHRIST
THE FIRST SUNDAY OF EPIPHANY

The 'Epiphany' (Greek *epiphaneia* – revealing, manifesting) is celebrated on 6 January. It refers to the revealing of the infant Christ to the 'Magi', the Wise Men from the East who discovered him to be the King of all the nations – Gentiles as well as Jews. That revelation was confirmed at Jesus' Baptism 30 years later when he was anointed with the Holy Spirit, and proclaimed the Son of God.

The Gathering

THE GREETING
May the light and peace of Jesus Christ our Lord be with you.
The Lord bless you.

(A HYMN may be sung)

THE CHRIST IS REVEALED TO THE MAGI
A star leads the Wise Men to the manger.

Arise, shine; for your light has come
**and the glory of the Lord
has risen upon you.**
Nations shall come to your light
and Kings to the brightness of your dawn.
They shall bring gold and frankincense
and shall proclaim the praise of the Lord.
(Isa. 60:1, 3, 6)

(Symbols of the Wise Men's gifts may be presented)

What gifts are fitting for Christ our Lord?

Bring gold for the King of the nations
who rules us in justice and peace.

Bring frankincense for the Son of God
who reveals the Father's love.

Bring myrrh for the Son of Man
who shared our sorrows and died for our sins.
Blessed be God for ever.

THE CHRIST IS REVEALED IN THE WATERS OF BAPTISM
This day Jesus is revealed as the Christ in the waters of Baptism.

I will take you from the nations:
and gather you from all the countries.

I will sprinkle clean water upon you:
and you shall be clean.

A new heart I will give you:
and a new spirit I will put within you.

You shall be my people:
and I will be your God. *(Ezek. 36:24ff.)*

(A flask of water may be placed centrally)

In his Baptism, Christ identified himself with sinful humanity. Through our Baptism, we are united with him, in his new Body, the Church.
Blessed be God for ever.

(The water may be taken to the Font)
(SONGS may be sung)
* * * * *

PENITENCE
The story of the Wise Men challenges us about our commitment to God:

When we have grown tired of searching for truth or seeking God's will,
Lord, have mercy.

When we have strayed from the command to love and serve our neighbour,
Christ, have mercy.

When we have offered less than the best in our worship and service of God,
Lord, have mercy.

May almighty God, who sent his Son into the world to save sinners, bring *us* his pardon and peace, now and for ever.
Amen.

(The GLORIA, the VENITE, a SONG or RESPONSES may be used)

THE COLLECT OF THE DAY
Let us pray … *(silent prayer)*

Eternal Father, who at the Baptism of Jesus revealed him to be your Son, anointing him with the Holy Spirit: grant to us, who are born again by water and the Spirit, that we may be faithful to our calling as your adopted children; through Jesus Christ your Son our Lord, who is alive and reigns with you, in the unity of the Holy Spirit, one God, now and for ever. **Amen.**

The Liturgy of the Word

THE SCRIPTURE READING(S)

(After the reading)
This is the Word of the Lord.
Thanks be to God.

PSALM/HYMN or SCRIPTURAL SONG

THE GOSPEL
Hear the Gospel of our Lord Jesus Christ according to N.
Glory to you, O Lord.

(After the reading)
This is the Gospel of the Lord.
Praise to you, O Christ.

THE SERMON

AFFIRMATION OF FAITH
At your Baptism you turned to Christ, repented of your sins, and renounced evil.

Do you now, at the start of a New Year, renew your allegiance to Christ?
We do, and with God's grace
we will follow him
as our Saviour and Lord.

Do you believe and trust in God the Father source of all being and life, the one for whom we exist?
We believe and trust in him.

Do you believe and trust in God the Son, who took our human nature, died for us and rose again?
We believe and trust in him.

Do you believe and trust in God the Holy Spirit, who gives life to the people of God and makes Christ known in the world?
We believe and trust in him.

This is the faith of the Church.
This is our faith.
We believe and trust in one God,
Father, Son and Holy Spirit. **Amen.**

(A HYMN may be sung)

The Prayers

INTERCESSIONS
(Special thanksgivings and prayers …)

The Wise Men offered gold to Christ, the King of all. Father, we pray for all who take authority to serve their country: our Queen, and the government of this and every nation … Give wisdom and integrity to all who lead, that their service will promote justice, peace and human well-being.
Your Kingdom come, **your will be done.**

The Wise Men offered frankincense to Christ, the Son of God. Father, we pray for the Church's life of worship and prayer, and for all who lead, teach and minister among us … Send the Holy Spirit to bless your servants with the gifts they need to build up the Body of Christ.
Your Kingdom come, **your will be done.**

The Wise Men offered myrrh to Christ, the Son of Man. Father, we pray for all who suffer from the injustices of life …
Bring deliverance to those who are trapped in grinding poverty, or brutal oppression … Strengthen your servants who go to help them. Be close to all who suffer from pain or ill-health … Grant healing and hope to them all.
Your Kingdom come, **your will be done.**

Father God, grant that we, with all who have lived and died in the faith of Christ, may share in his eternal Kingdom. **Amen.**

THE LORD'S PRAYER

(A HYMN may be sung)

CONCLUDING PRAYER
May God the Father, the rock of our salvation, who has brought us to birth as his children, by the water of Baptism and the Spirit of Life, keep us faithful to our calling as followers of our Saviour, Jesus Christ.
Amen.

(THE BLESSING or THE GRACE is said)

THE SECOND SUNDAY OF EPIPHANY
'God makes known his glory in lives renewed by Christ'

The 'Epiphany season' began on 6 January with the celebration of the Wise Men's visit to Bethlehem where Christ was revealed to them as the King of all nations. During the following four weeks of the season the Sunday readings remind us of the different ways Christ's glory was revealed to other people of his time.

The Gathering

THE GREETING
The Lord of glory be with you.
The Lord bless you.

(A HYMN may be sung)

May God be gracious to us and bless us,
and make his face to shine upon us:

that your way may be known upon earth,
your saving power among all nations:

let the peoples praise you, O God:
let all the peoples praise you.
                                        (Ps. 67:1-3)

PRAYER
Almighty God,
to whom all hearts are open,
all desires known, and from whom
no secrets are hidden:
cleanse the thoughts of our hearts
by the inspiration of your Holy Spirit,
that we may perfectly love you,
and worthily magnify your holy name;
through Christ our Lord.   *Amen.*

(SONGS may be sung)
* * * * *

PENITENCE
During the season of Epiphany, let us seek the renewal of our lives in the light of God's love for us, revealed by Jesus Christ:

Jesus, Saviour of all, who revealed the breadth of God's love, forgive us when we fail to show care to those who are different.
Lord, have mercy.   **Lord, have mercy.**

Jesus, Son of God, who revealed the depth of God's love, forgive us when we are too busy to pray, or to seek God's will.
Christ, have mercy.   **Christ, have mercy.**

Jesus, Son of Man, who revealed the cost of God's love, forgive us when we have made light of our sins.
Lord, have mercy.   **Lord, have mercy.**

May Almighty God have mercy on *us*, forgive *us our* sins, and bring *us* to everlasting life, through Jesus Christ our Lord.   **Amen.**

(The GLORIA, the VENITE, a SONG or RESPONSES may be used)

THE COLLECT OF THE DAY
Let us pray …   *(silent prayer)*

Almighty God,
in Christ you make all things new: transform the poverty of our nature by the riches of your grace, and in the renewal of our lives make known your heavenly glory; through Jesus Christ your Son our Lord, who is alive and reigns with you, in the unity of the Holy Spirit, one God, now and forever.   **Amen.**

The Liturgy of the Word

THE SCRIPTURE READING(S)

(after the reading)
This is the Word of the Lord.
Thanks be to God.

PSALM/HYMN or SCRIPTURAL SONG

THE GOSPEL:
Hear the Gospel of our Lord Jesus Christ according to N.
Glory to you, O Lord.

(After the reading)
This is the Gospel of the Lord.
Praise to you, O Christ.

THE SERMON

AFFIRMATION OF FAITH

I believe in God, the Father almighty, creator of heaven and earth.
I believe in Jesus Christ, his only Son, our Lord, who was conceived by the Holy Spirit, born of the Virgin Mary, suffered under Pontius Pilate, was crucified, died and was buried; he descended to the dead. On the third day he rose again; he ascended into heaven, he is seated at the right hand of the Father, and he will come to judge the living and the dead.
I believe in the Holy Spirit, the holy catholic Church, the communion of saints, the forgiveness of sins, the resurrection of the body, and the life everlasting. **Amen.**
(The Apostles' Creed)

(A HYMN may be sung)

The Prayers

INTERCESSIONS

(Special thanksgivings and prayers …)

God, our heavenly Father, we give thanks that through your Son, Jesus Christ, new life and light, forgiveness and grace, have pierced the darkness of the world.
We pray for his Church, especially each other here, and those who minister among us …
Send the Holy Spirit to unite us in worship, nourish us with truth, and strengthen us as witnesses of Christ in our daily lives.
God be gracious to us **and bless us.**

We pray for all who take authority: our Queen and government and the leaders of other nations … Enlighten the minds of those who lead, that their decisions may bring justice for the oppressed, peace for those at war, and the well-being of all.
God be gracious to us **and bless us.**

We pray for all who live and work in this neighbourhood, and all who serve its needs … Give us such love for you that we may offer our time and talents in the service of others and in building community life.
God be gracious to us **and bless us.**

We pray for those who are facing ill-health or old age, disability or personal tragedy …
Grant them encouragement, and give grace to all who bring care and healing.
God be gracious to us **and bless us.**

We remember with thanksgiving those who have died … Grant us with them, (with N.) and with all the saints, a share in your eternal Kingdom, through Jesus Christ our Lord. **Amen.**

THE LORD'S PRAYER

(A HYMN may be sung)

CONCLUDING PRAYER

Christ our Lord, to whom kings bowed down in worship, reveal your glory to us, and strengthen us to serve you in all the world. **Amen.**

(THE BLESSING or THE GRACE is said)

THE THIRD SUNDAY OF EPIPHANY
'Renew your people with your heavenly grace'

During the four weeks of the 'Epiphany season' the Sunday Gospel readings describe the first encounters Jesus had with various people, in which he revealed who he was and the purpose of his coming. Sometimes these encounters were accompanied by 'signs and miracles' (as today's Collect says). But always they led to the 'renewing' and 'sustaining' of lives that were aimless or frail.

The Gathering

THE GREETING
The Lord of glory be with you.
The Lord bless you.

(A HYMN may be sung)

The Lord is my light and my salvation; whom shall I fear?
The Lord is the stronghold of my life; of whom shall I be afraid?

I believe that I shall see the goodness of the Lord in the land of the living.
Wait for the Lord: be strong, and let your heart take courage; wait for the Lord!
(Ps. 27:1, 13-14)

PRAYER
Almighty God,
to whom all hearts are open,
all desires known, and from whom
no secrets are hidden:
cleanse the thoughts of our hearts
by the inspiration of your Holy Spirit,
that we may perfectly love you,
and worthily magnify your holy name;
through Christ our Lord.   Amen.

(SONGS may be sung)
* * * * *

PENITENCE
During the season of Epiphany, let us seek the renewal of our lives in the light of God's love for us, revealed by Jesus Christ:

Jesus, Saviour of all, who revealed the breadth of God's love, forgive us when we fail to show care to those who are different.
Lord, have mercy.   ***Lord, have mercy.***

Jesus, Son of God, who revealed the depth of God's love, forgive us when we are too busy to pray, or to seek God's will.
Christ, have mercy.   ***Christ, have mercy.***

Jesus, Son of Man, who revealed the cost of God's love, forgive us when we have made light of our sins.
Lord, have mercy.   ***Lord, have mercy.***

May Almighty God have mercy on *us*, forgive *us our* sins, and bring *us* to everlasting life, through Jesus Christ our Lord.   ***Amen.***

(The GLORIA, the VENITE, a SONG or RESPONSES may be used)

THE COLLECT OF THE DAY
Let us pray …   *(silent prayer)*

Almighty God,
whose Son revealed in signs and miracles the wonder of your saving presence: renew your people with your heavenly grace, and in all our weakness sustain us by your mighty power, through Jesus Christ your Son our Lord, who is alive and reigns with you, in the unity of the Holy Spirit, one God, now and for ever.   ***Amen.***

The Liturgy of the Word

THE SCRIPTURE READING(S)

(after the reading)
This is the Word of the Lord.
Thanks be to God.

PSALM/HYMN or SCRIPTURAL SONG

THE GOSPEL
Hear the Gospel of our Lord Jesus Christ according to N.
Glory to you, O Lord.

(After the reading)
This is the Gospel of the Lord.
Praise to you, O Christ.

THE SERMON

AFFIRMATION OF FAITH
Let us declare our faith in God:

Do you believe and trust in God the Father,
source of all being and life,
the one for whom we exist?
We believe and trust in him.

Do you believe and trust in God the Son,
who took our human nature,
died for us and rose again?
We believe and trust in him.

Do you believe and trust in God the Holy Spirit, who gives life to the people of God and makes Christ known in the world?
We believe and trust in him.

This is the faith of the Church.
**This is our faith.
We believe and trust in one God,
Father, Son and Holy Spirit.** Amen.

(A HYMN may be sung)

The Prayers

INTERCESSIONS
(Special thanksgivings and prayers ...)

God, our Father, we hold before you the needs of your people:
we pray for all who share in the fellowship of Christ's Church: for bishop N. and the work of this diocese ... for all who teach and minister among us; for each other here and the life of this church ... for our fellow Christians in other places ... Fill us with the Holy Spirit that we may grow strong in faith, hope and love.
Lord, in your mercy, **hear our prayer.**

We pray for our country: for our Queen and government ... for other nations and their leaders ... for people suffering from violence or disasters ... Give wisdom and integrity to those who lead that they may promote justice, peace and the well-being of all.
Lord, in your mercy, **hear our prayer.**

We pray for all amongst whom we live and work: for our neighbours and friends ... for workmates or clients ... for those who serve our community ... Make us more aware of each other's situation, and more eager to help out.
Lord, in your mercy, **hear our prayer.**

We pray for those whose bodies or minds are hurting: the ill or frail, the injured or disabled, the lonely or bereaved ... Grant healing through the skills of doctors and nurses, and through the care of family and friends.
Lord, in your mercy, **hear our prayer.**

We remember with thanksgiving those who have died ... Grant us with them, (with N.) and with all the saints, a share in your eternal Kingdom, through Christ our Lord.
Amen.

THE LORD'S PRAYER

(A HYMN may be sung)

CONCLUDING PRAYER
Christ our Lord, to whom kings knelt down in worship, reveal your glory to us, send down the riches of your grace and strengthen us to serve you in all the world. Amen.

(THE BLESSING or THE GRACE is said)

THE FOURTH SUNDAY OF EPIPHANY
'The knowledge of God's glory – revealed in Christ'

As we draw to the end of the 'Epiphany season' we are reminded that our knowledge of God arises not from our own spiritual search, but from God revealing himself to us. The season began with the revelation to the Wise Men that his rule on earth was now focused in a vulnerable young child named Jesus. Today's Collect prays that this 'glorious gospel may dispel ignorance ... and reveal ... God's glory.'

The Gathering

THE GREETING
The Lord of glory be with you.
The Lord bless you.

(A HYMN may be sung)

How precious is your steadfast love, O God!
All people may take refuge in the shadow of your wings.

They feast on the abundance of your house,
and you give them drink from the river of your delights.

For with you is the fountain of life;
in your light we see light.
(Ps. 36:7-9)

PRAYER
***O Lord,
open our eyes to see what is beautiful,
our minds to know what is true,
and our hearts to seek what is good,
for Jesus' sake.*** Amen.

(SONGS may be sung)

* * * * *

PENITENCE
During the season of Epiphany, let us seek the renewal of our lives in the light of God's love for us, revealed by Jesus Christ:

Jesus, Saviour of all, who revealed the extent of God's love, forgive us when we limit our care only to those we find congenial. **Lord, have mercy.**

Jesus, Son of God, who revealed the closeness of God's love, forgive us when we are too busy to pray, or to seek God's will.
Christ, have mercy.

Jesus, Son of Man, who revealed the cost of God's love, forgive us when we have made light of our sins. **Lord, have mercy.**

Let us confess all our sins in penitence and faith:
Almighty God, our heavenly Father, we have sinned against you and against our neighbour in thought and word and deed, through negligence, through weakness, through our own deliberate fault. We are truly sorry and repent of all our sins. For the sake of your Son Jesus Christ, who died for us, forgive us all that is past and grant that we may serve you in newness of life to the glory of your name. Amen.

May almighty God have mercy on *us*, forgive *us* our sins,
and bring *us* to everlasting life,
through Jesus Christ our Lord. **Amen.**

(The GLORIA, the VENITE, a SONG or RESPONSES may be used)

THE COLLECT OF THE DAY
Let us pray ... *(silent prayer)*

God our Creator,
who in the beginning commanded the light to shine out of darkness: we pray that the light of the glorious gospel of Christ may dispel the darkness of ignorance and unbelief, shine into the hearts of all your people, and reveal the knowledge of your glory in the face of Jesus Christ your Son our Lord, who is alive and reigns with you in the unity of the Holy Spirit, one God, now and for ever.
Amen.

The Liturgy of the Word

THE SCRIPTURE READING(S)

(After the reading)
This is the Word of the Lord.
Thanks be to God.

PSALM/HYMN or SCRIPTURAL SONG

THE GOSPEL
Hear the Gospel of our Lord Jesus Christ according to N.
Glory to you, O Lord.

(After the reading)
This is the Gospel of the Lord.
Praise to you, O Christ.

THE SERMON

AFFIRMATION OF FAITH
Let us declare our faith in God:

Do you believe and trust in God the Father, source of all being and life, the one for whom we exist?
We believe and trust in him.

Do you believe and trust in God the Son, who took our human nature,
died for us and rose again?
We believe and trust in him.

Do you believe and trust in God the Holy Spirit, who gives life to the people of God and makes Christ known in the world?
We believe and trust in him.

This is the faith of the Church.
This is our faith.
We believe and trust in one God,
Father, Son and Holy Spirit.
                                                                    Amen.

(A HYMN may be sung)

The Prayers

INTERCESSIONS
(Special thanksgivings and prayers ...)

God our Father, we pray for your blessing on all people:
Bless our Queen and those who govern the nations ... that they may rule with wisdom and integrity, and bring justice and peace to the world:
Jesus, Lord of all,   ***in your mercy hear us.***

Bless those who minister in Christ's Church that they may be firm in faith, clear in vision yet humble in your service:
Jesus, Lord of all,   ***in your mercy hear us.***

Bless those who teach, that they may increase our understanding of the faith, and listen to your word for them:
Jesus, Lord of all,   ***in your mercy hear us.***

Bless those who have demanding work to do ... that they may use their gifts for the common good, and bear witness to Christ in the service they render:
Jesus, Lord of all,   ***in your mercy hear us.***

Bless those who suffer from ill-health, unremitting pain, or loneliness ... Bring them out of their distress and grant them your peace:
Jesus, Lord of all,   ***in your mercy hear us.***

Bless those who care for the sick and frail ... that they may bring strength and encouragement to others, yet know your healing in themselves.
Jesus, Lord of all,   ***in your mercy hear us.***

We remember with thanksgiving those who have died ...
Jesus, Lord of all, grant us with them a share in your eternal Kingdom.   Amen.

THE LORD'S PRAYER

(A HYMN may be sung)

CONCLUDING PRAYER
Christ our Lord,
to whom kings knelt down in worship,
reveal your glory to us,
and strengthen us to serve you in all the world.   Amen.

(The BLESSING or the GRACE is said)

THE PRESENTATION OF CHRIST IN THE TEMPLE

'CANDLEMAS'

When Mary and Joseph presented their son to God, Simeon and Anna, representing all faithful Jews, recognized him as both Israel's Saviour and the one who would 'enlighten the Gentiles'. This festival may be celebrated by processing with lighted candles, symbolizing Christ, the True Light. Held on or near 2nd February, it closes the Epiphany season, but the sombre words of Simeon hint at sufferings to come.

The Gathering

THE GREETING
The Lord of glory be with you.
The Lord bless you.

(A HYMN may be sung)

In Jesus was life
and the life was the light of all people.

The light shines in the darkness
and the darkness did not overcome it.

The true light, which enlightens everyone
was coming into the world.
(John 1:4-5, 9)

(SONGS may be sung)

* * * * *

PENITENCE
Jesus says, 'I am the light of the world. Whoever follows me will never walk in darkness, but will have the light of life.'
(John 8:12)

Let us then examine our lives in his light and confess our sins in penitence and faith.
**Almighty God, our heavenly Father,
we have sinned against you
and against our neighbour,
in thought and word and deed,
through negligence, through weakness,
through our own deliberate fault.
We are truly sorry,
and repent of all our sins.
For the sake of your Son Jesus Christ,
who died for us,
forgive us all that is past,
and grant that we may serve you
in newness of life
to the glory of your name.** Amen.

May Almighty God have mercy on *us*,
forgive *us our* sins, and bring *us* to everlasting life,
through Jesus Christ our Lord. **Amen.**

(The GLORIA, the VENITE, a SONG or RESPONSES may be used)

THE COLLECT OF THE DAY
Let us pray ...   *(silent prayer)*

Almighty and ever-living God, clothed in majesty, whose beloved Son was this day presented in the Temple, in substance of our flesh: grant that we may be presented to you with pure and clean hearts, by your Son Jesus Christ our Lord, who is alive and reigns with you, in the unity of the Holy Spirit, one God, now and forever.
Amen.

The Liturgy of the Word

THE SCRIPTURE READING(S)

(After the reading)
This is the word of the Lord.
Thanks be to God.

PSALM/HYMN or SCRIPTURAL SONG

THE GOSPEL
Hear the Gospel of our Lord Jesus Christ according to N.
Glory to you, O Lord.

(After the reading)
This is the Gospel of the Lord.
Praise to you, O Christ.

Today the Lord is presented in the Temple in substance of our mortal nature. *Alleluia!*
Today the Blessed Virgin comes to be purified in accordance with the law. *Alleluia!*
Today old Simeon proclaims Christ as the light of the nations and the glory of Israel. *Alleluia!*
Praise to Christ, the Light of the world!

THE SERMON

AFFIRMATION OF FAITH

Do you believe and trust in God the Father, source of all being and life, the one for whom we exist?
We believe and trust in him.

Do you believe and trust in God the Son, who took our human nature, died for us and rose again?
We believe and trust in him.

Do you believe and trust in God the Holy Spirit,
who gives life to the people of God and makes Christ known in the world?
We believe and trust in him.

This is the faith of the Church.
**This is our faith.
We believe and trust in one God,
Father, Son and Holy Spirit. Amen.**

(A HYMN may be sung)

The Prayers

INTERCESSIONS

(Special thanksgivings and prayers ...)

Recalling how the infant Jesus was brought to the Temple to be presented to God, we pray for all who bring their children to church for baptism, or dedication, or instruction ... God our Father, bless the work of this church among children and young people, that they will grow in faith.
Christ, Light of the world, **shine upon us.**

Giving thanks for Simeon's good and holy life, we pray for all who serve Christ today: for bishop *N.* and the work of this diocese ... for all who teach and minister among us ... for each other here, and the life of our church ... Renew us all with the Holy Spirit.
Christ, Light of the world, **shine upon us.**

Giving thanks that Simeon recognized Jesus as his Saviour, we pray for all who are searching for God ... for those in enquirer groups, confirmation classes or Bible study groups ... Deepen our knowledge of the faith.
Christ, Light of the world, **shine upon us.**

Remembering Simeon's prophecy about the opposition Jesus would face, we pray for all who are persecuted today for their Christian faith ... Sustain them as they bear witness among hostile people, and save them from the powers of evil.
Christ, Light of the world, **shine upon us.**

Giving thanks for Anna's long and faithful life of prayer, we pray for all who, like her, suffer the distress of bereavement, old age or human frailty ... Grant to all in need, the encouragement to keep going, and the healing that they long for.
Christ, Light of the world, **shine upon us.**

We remember those who have died ...
May light perpetual shine upon them.
Heavenly Father, grant all these prayers for the sake of Jesus Christ our Lord. **Amen.**

THE LORD'S PRAYER

*(A HYMN may be sung; candles may be lit
THE SONG OF SIMEON - 'Nunc Dimittis' - may be said or sung; a CANDLEMAS procession may proceed to the Font)*

**Now, Lord, you let your servant go in peace: your word has been fulfilled.
My own eyes have seen the salvation which you have prepared in the sight of every people;
a light to reveal you to the nations and the glory of your people Israel.**

CONCLUDING PRAYER

Now we turn from celebrating Christ's birth, to confronting the darkness he came to dispel.
Let us follow him so that we never walk in darkness, but have the light of life. Amen.

(THE BLESSING or THE GRACE is said)

THE FIFTH SUNDAY BEFORE LENT
'Called to serve; made worthy of our calling'

The Sundays before Lent are an in-between phase in the Church Calendar, sometimes also called 'ordinary time' because no special season or theme occurs in it. The celebrations of Christmas and Epiphany are behind us, and Lent is not far ahead. In the meantime, we seek to live as servants of the God who, as today's Collect puts it, forgives and accepts us in Christ, and calls us to serve him.

The Gathering

THE GREETING
Grace, mercy and peace from God our Father and the Lord Jesus Christ be with you.
And also with you. (1 Tim. 1:2)
(A HYMN may be sung)

Create in me a clean heart, O God,
and put a new and right spirit within me.

Do not cast me away from your presence,
and do not take your Holy Spirit from me.

Restore to me the joy of your salvation,
and sustain in me a willing spirit.

O Lord, open my lips
and my mouth will declare your praise.
(Ps, 51:11, 12-18)

PRAYER
Almighty God, to whom all hearts are open, all desires known, and from whom no secrets are hidden: cleanse the thoughts of our hearts by the inspiration of your Holy Spirit, that we may perfectly love you, and worthily magnify your holy name; through Christ our Lord. **Amen.**

(SONGS may be sung)

* * * * *

PENITENCE
In a moment of quiet, let us reflect on our lives, and confess to God those selfish attitudes that have led us into sin against God and neighbour …

Hear what St Paul says: 'The saying is sure and worthy of full acceptance, that Christ Jesus came into the world to save sinners.'
(1 Tim. 1:15)

Let us confess all our sins in penitence and faith:

Almighty God, our heavenly Father, we have sinned against you and against our neighbour in thought and word and deed, through negligence, through weakness, through our own deliberate fault.
We are truly sorry and repent of all our sins. For the sake of your Son Jesus Christ, who died for us, forgive us all that is past and grant that we may serve you in newness of life to the glory of your name. **Amen.**

May almighty God have mercy on *us*,
forgive *us* our sins,
and bring *us* to everlasting life,
through Jesus Christ our Lord. **Amen.**

(The GLORIA, the VENITE, a SONG or RESPONSES may be used)

THE COLLECT OF THE DAY
Let us pray … (silent prayer)

Almighty God,
by whose grace alone we are accepted and called to your service:
strengthen us by your Holy Spirit
and make us worthy of our calling;
through Jesus Christ your Son our Lord,
who is alive and reigns with you,
in the unity of the Holy Spirit,
one God, now and for ever. **Amen.**

The Liturgy of the Word

THE SCRIPTURE READING(S)

(After the reading)
This is the Word of the Lord.
Thanks be to God.

PSALM, HYMN or SCRIPTURAL SONG

THE GOSPEL

Hear the Gospel of our Lord Jesus Christ according to N.
Glory to you, O .Lord.

(After the reading)
This is the Gospel of the Lord.
Praise to you, O Christ.

THE SERMON

AFFIRMATION OF FAITH

Let us declare our faith in God:

Do you believe and trust in God the Father, source of all being and life, the one for whom we exist?
We believe and trust in him.

Do you believe and trust in God the Son, who took our human nature, died for us and rose again?
We believe and trust in him.

Do you believe and trust in God the Holy Spirit, who gives life to the people of God and makes Christ known in the world?
We believe and trust in him.

This is the faith of the Church.
This is our faith.
We believe and trust in one God, Father, Son and Holy Spirit. Amen.

(A HYMN may be sung)

The Prayers

INTERCESSIONS

(Special thanksgivings and prayers …)

Friends and followers of Jesus, we have come together because of his love for us and our faith in him. Let us now pray for all who need the strength and guidance of God's Spirit in meeting the challenges that life brings.

For bishop N. and for all church ministers, clergy and lay, that they will serve in humility and holiness …
Jesus, Lord and Saviour,
(R:) Send the Holy Spirit upon us.

For our Queen and government and the leaders of other nations, that they will promote peace and justice, freedom and opportunity …
Jesus, Lord and Saviour, **(R:)**

For those places in the world where food is scarce, jobs are few or life is dangerous, that the strong will help the weak in their struggle for a better life …
Jesus, Lord and Saviour, **(R:)**

For the needy and vulnerable in our own neighbourhood, that we may respond to their plight with compassion and practical care …
Jesus, Lord and Saviour, **(R:)**

For our families and all who are close to us, that in times of trial they will be protected from harm and make the right choices …
Jesus, Lord and Saviour, **(R:)**

For all who face disability or chronic illness, that they may have encouragement in coping with their difficulties …
Jesus, Lord and Saviour, **(R:)**

For those who are ill, in pain, or undergoing treatment, that they will be healed and restored to a better quality of life …
Jesus, Lord and Saviour, **(R:)**

For those in darkness and grief because they are parted from someone they love, that they will be comforted, and lifted by hope …
Jesus, Lord and Saviour, **answer all the prayers we offer according to your will.**
Amen.

THE LORD'S PRAYER

(A HYMN may be sung)

CONCLUDING PRAYER

Lord Jesus Christ, redeemer, friend and brother: **may we know you more clearly, love you more dearly, and follow you more nearly, day by day.** Amen.
(St Richard of Chichester)

(The BLESSING or the GRACE is said)

THE FOURTH SUNDAY BEFORE LENT
'Supported in all dangers and carried through all temptations'

In the Church Calendar the Sundays before Lent are known as 'ordinary time' because no special season or theme occurs in this period. However, we still need God's help to follow the Christian way when life is 'ordinary' because dangers and temptations are as present as ever. Today's Collect prays that God's strength and protection will carry us through such times.

The Gathering

THE GREETING
The grace and mercy of our Lord Jesus Christ be with you. *(1 Tim. 1:2)*
And also with you.

(A HYMN may be sung)

I will give thanks to the Lord with my whole heart,
I will tell of all your wonderful deeds.

I will be glad and exult in you:
**I will sing praise to your name,
O Most High.** *(Ps. 9:1-2)*

PRAYER
**God our Father,
we have gathered here to celebrate your love for us. Help us to worship you with all our hearts,
to seek you with all our minds,
to long for you with all our souls,
and to follow you with all our strength,
through Jesus Christ our Lord. Amen.**

(SONGS may be sung)

* * * * *

PENITENCE
In a moment of quiet reflection, we lay aside all pretence towards God and lay before him our self-centred lives, and the hurt we often inflict on others ...

Let us confess our sins in penitence and faith.
**Almighty God, our heavenly Father,
we have sinned against you
and against our neighbour
in thought and word and deed,
through negligence, through weakness,
through our own deliberate fault.
We are truly sorry
and repent of all our sins.
For the sake of your Son Jesus Christ,
who died for us,
forgive us all that is past and grant that
we may serve you in newness of life
to the glory of your name. Amen.**

Almighty God,
who forgives all who truly repent,
have mercy upon *us*,
pardon and deliver *us* from all *our* sins,
confirm and strengthen *us* in all goodness,
and keep *us* in life eternal;
through Jesus Christ our Lord. **Amen.**

(The GLORIA, the VENITE, a SONG or RESPONSES may be used)

THE COLLECT OF THE DAY
Let us pray ... *(silent prayer)*

O God,
you know us to be set in the midst of so many and great dangers, that by reason of the frailty of our nature we cannot always stand upright:
grant to us such strength and protection as may support us in all dangers
and carry us through all temptations;
through Jesus Christ your Son our Lord,
who is alive and reigns with you,
in the unity of the Holy Spirit,
one God, now and for ever. **Amen.**

The Liturgy of the Word

THE SCRIPTURE READING(S)

(After the reading)
This is the Word of the Lord.
Thanks be to God.

PSALM/HYMN or SCRIPTURAL SONG

THE GOSPEL
Hear the Gospel of our Lord Jesus Christ according to N.
Glory to you, O Lord.

(After the reading)
This is the Gospel of the Lord.
Praise to you, O Christ.

THE SERMON

AFFIRMATION OF FAITH
Let us affirm our faith in God:

I believe in God, the Father almighty, creator of heaven and earth.

I believe in Jesus Christ, his only Son, our Lord,
who was conceived by the Holy Spirit,
born of the Virgin Mary,
suffered under Pontius Pilate,
was crucified, died and was buried;
he descended to the dead.
On the third day he rose again;
he ascended into heaven,
he is seated at the right hand of the Father and he will come to judge the living and the dead.

I believe in the Holy Spirit,
the holy catholic Church,
the communion of saints,
the forgiveness of sins,
the resurrection of the body,
and the life everlasting. **Amen.**

(A HYMN may be sung)

The Prayers

INTERCESSIONS
(Special thanksgivings and prayers ...)

Our Father in heaven, we give thanks for the Church and for all that we receive through its worship, teaching and fellowship. We pray:

for bishop N. and the life of this diocese ...
for each other here and all who minister among us ...
for our fellow Christians in other places ...
Renew us with the Holy Spirit that we may bear witness to Christ's love.
Lord, in your mercy, **hear our prayer.**

We give thanks for this nation and those in authority who serve the people with integrity and dedication. We pray:
for our Queen and government ...
for all who work in the media ...
for those suffering from disaster, war or oppression ...
Bring justice and harmony to all people, and new opportunities to make the most of their lives.
Lord, in your mercy, **hear our prayer.**

We give thanks for our community, for all who serve us, and those who cherish us ...
Strengthen the bonds of trust and respect within families, communities and workplaces
Lord, in your mercy, **hear our prayer.**

We give thanks for the health we have, and for the skills of those who attend to us when we are in need. Bring healing and encouragement to those suffering from ill-health, pain or frailty ...
Lord, in your mercy, **hear our prayer.**

We give thanks for those who have died and those whose memory is still treasured ...
Grant us, with them, and with all the saints ... the joy of eternal life in Christ, our Lord.
Amen.

THE LORD'S PRAYER

(A HYMN may be sung)

CONCLUDING PRAYER
May the God of hope fill us with
all joy and peace in believing,
by the power of the Holy Spirit. **Amen.**
(Rom. 15:13)

(THE BLESSING or THE GRACE is said)

THE THIRD SUNDAY BEFORE LENT
'Love what God commands, desire what he promises'

Although the Sundays before Lent are called 'ordinary time' because no special season or theme occurs in this period, most of us find that life seldom seems ordinary. Today's Collect mentions the 'unruly wills and passions of sinful humanity' interacting with 'the many changes of this world'. It prays for grace to fix our hearts on 'true joys', by loving what God commands and desiring what he promises.

The Gathering

THE GREETING
Grace to you and peace from God our Father and the Lord Jesus Christ.
And also with you. (Rom. 1:7)

(A HYMN may be sung)

Happy are those
who do not follow the advice of the wicked
*or take the path that sinners tread,
or sit in the seat of scoffers;*

but their delight is in the law of the Lord,
*and on his law
they meditate day and night,*

they are like trees planted by streams of water, which yield their fruit in its season, and their leaves do not wither.
in all that they do, they prosper.
(Ps. 1:1-3)

PRAYER
*Let the words of my mouth
and the meditation of my heart
be acceptable to you,
O Lord, my rock and my redeemer.
Amen.* (Ps. 19:14)

(SONGS may be sung)

* * * * *

PENITENCE
In a moment of quiet reflection, we lay aside all pretence towards God and lay before him our self-centred lives, and the hurt we often inflict on others ...

Let us confess our sins in penitence and faith.

*Almighty God, our heavenly Father,
we have sinned against you
and against our neighbour
in thought and word and deed,
through negligence, through weakness,
through our own deliberate fault.
We are truly sorry
and repent of all our sins.
For the sake of your Son Jesus Christ,
who died for us,
forgive us all that is past and grant that
we may serve you in newness of life
to the glory of your name.   Amen.*

May Almighty God have mercy on *us*,
forgive *us* our sins,
and bring *us* to everlasting life,
through Jesus Christ our Lord.   **Amen.**

(The GLORIA, the VENITE, a SONG or RESPONSES may be used)

THE COLLECT OF THE DAY
Let us pray ...   *(silent prayer)*

Almighty God,
who alone can bring order to the unruly wills and passions of sinful humanity: give your people grace so to love what you command and to desire what you promise, that, among the many changes of this world, our hearts may surely there be fixed where true joys are to be found;
through Jesus Christ your Son our Lord,
who is alive and reigns with you,
in the unity of the Holy Spirit,
one God, now and for ever.   **Amen.**

The Liturgy of the Word

THE SCRIPTURE READING(S)

(After the reading)
This is the Word of the Lord.
Thanks be to God.

PSALM/HYMN or SCRIPTURAL SONG

THE GOSPEL
Hear the Gospel of our Lord Jesus Christ according to N.
Glory to you, O lord.

(After the reading)
This is the Gospel of the Lord.
Praise to you, O Christ.

THE SERMON

AFFIRMATION OF FAITH
Let us declare faith in God:
I believe in God, the Father almighty, creator of heaven and earth.
I believe in Jesus Christ, his only Son, our Lord, who was conceived by the Holy Spirit, born of the Virgin Mary, suffered under Pontius Pilate, was crucified, died and was buried; he descended to the dead. On the third day he rose again; he ascended into heaven, he is seated at the right hand of the Father and he will come to judge the living and the dead.

I believe in the Holy Spirit, the holy catholic Church, the communion of saints, the forgiveness of sins, the resurrection of the body, and the life everlasting. Amen.
(The Apostles' Creed)

(A HYMN may be sung)

The Prayers

INTERCESSIONS

(Special thanksgivings and prayers ...)

Father God, who knows our needs before we ask, hear our prayers for all people:

Give grace to those who minister in your Church: Bishop N., the clergy and all lay ministers ... Anoint them with the Spirit for their work in building up the body of Christ.
Lord in your mercy, ***hear our prayer.***

Sustain our Christian brothers and sisters in other places who are persecuted ... Deliver those who are in prison for their beliefs.
Lord, in your mercy, ***hear our prayer.***

Guide our Queen and government and the leaders of the nations in all their decisions ... Bring reconciliation to situations where there is deep and bitter conflict, and new opportunities for all to make the most of their lives.
Lord, in your mercy, ***hear our prayer.***

Enlighten all who are engaged in scientific research. May their work promote the life, health and well-being of the world.
Lord, in your mercy, ***hear our prayer.***

Bless the work of our local schools ... Give teachers the skill, enthusiasm and patience to inspire the young to learn.
Lord, in your mercy, ***hear our prayer.***

Be with those whose work is very demanding or unrewarding ... Give employers understanding of their needs.
Lord, in your mercy, ***hear our prayer.***

Be close to those who are unwell, frail or disabled ... Bless all who bring healing and care, and who sustain hope.
Lord, in your mercy, ***hear our prayer.***

We remember with thanksgiving those who have died ... Strengthen all who grieve, with comfort, faith and peace, for Jesus' sake.
Amen.

THE LORD'S PRAYER

(A HYMN may be sung)

CONCLUDING PRAYER
Go before us, Lord, in all we do with your most gracious favour, and guide us with your continual help, that in all our works begun, continued and ended in you, we may glorify your holy name, and finally by your mercy receive everlasting life; through Christ our Lord. ***Amen.***
(Collect from Common Worship)

(THE BLESSING or THE GRACE is said)

THE SECOND SUNDAY BEFORE LENT
'God the Creator'

On the Second Sunday before Lent the Church celebrates God's creation. We give thanks for its breath-taking grandeur, its intricate design and its abundant life – all signs of a wise and loving Creator. This earth is God's gift to us, the 'home' which we share with all living creatures, and which we look after as God's stewards, 'in his image' – as the Bible, and as today's Collect, define human nature.

The Gathering

THE GREETING
Grace to you, and peace from God our Father and the Lord Jesus Christ be with you.
And also with you. *(Rom. 1:7)*

(A HYMN may be sung)

(Images may be displayed, or objects brought forward, to represent different aspects of creation:)

O God, immense like a desert plain,
we cannot see to the ends of you.

O God, tall like the mountains,
you rise beyond our limited vision.

O God, vast like the ocean,
we cannot plumb your depths.

O God, rich like the fertile soil,
we depend on your gifts.

O God, glorious like the flowers of the field,
we delight in the beauty of creation.

O God, giver of life to all creatures great and small,
we rejoice to share this vibrant earth with them.

O God, loving us more than any parent could,
we trust in your amazing grace.

O Lord,
**open our eyes to see what is beautiful,
our minds to know what is true,
and our hearts to seek what is good,
for Jesus' sake.** ***Amen.***

(SONGS may be sung)

* * * * *

PENITENCE
In a moment of quiet, let us think about the selfish ways in which human beings exploit the gifts of the earth …

We confess our sins to God our Creator:

For the greed and excess that deplete the natural resources of the world,
Lord, have mercy.

For the uncaring attitudes that allow pollution to spread relentlessly, even into the air we breathe,
Christ, have mercy.

For the arrogance that makes creation serve human desires without regard to the suffering caused, or the delicate balance of Nature,
Lord, have mercy.

The almighty and merciful Lord grant *us* pardon and forgiveness of all *our* sins, time for amendment of life, and the grace and strength of the Holy Spirit. ***Amen.***

(The GLORIA, the VENITE, a SONG or RESPONSES may be used)

THE COLLECT OF THE DAY
Let us pray … *(silent prayer)*

Almighty God, you have created the heavens and the earth and made us in your own image: teach us to discern your hand in all your works and your likeness in all your children; through Jesus Christ your Son our Lord, who with you and the Holy Spirit reigns supreme over all things, now and for ever.
Amen.

The Liturgy of the Word

THE SCRIPTURE READING(S)

(After the reading)
This is the Word of the Lord.
Thanks be to God.

PSALM/HYMN or SONG OF CREATION ('The Benedicite')

THE GOSPEL
Hear the Gospel of our Lord Jesus Christ according to N.
Glory to you, O Lord.

(After the reading)
This is the Gospel of the Lord.
Praise to you, O Christ.

THE SERMON

AFFIRMATION OF FAITH
Let us declare our faith in God:

Do you believe and trust in God the Father, source of all being and life, the one for whom we exist?
We believe and trust in him.

Do you believe and trust in God the Son, who took our human nature,
died for us and rose again?
We believe and trust in him.

Do you believe and trust in God the Holy Spirit, who gives life to the people of God and makes Christ known in the world?
We believe and trust in him.

This is the faith of the Church.
This is our faith.
We believe and trust in one God,
Father, Son and Holy Spirit. **Amen.**

(A HYMN may be sung)

The Prayers

INTERCESSIONS

Creator God, you have provided us with a beautiful world to live in, so abundant with life and opportunity, yet fragile and now so damaged:
- help us to be your stewards who look after this, our earthly home …
- teach us to care for the rivers, the forests and the wild places …
- save us from the greed that consumes more and more …
- guide us to find ways of producing things that do not pollute the earth with litter, waste and poisonous substances
- give us respect and compassion for all animals …

Creator God, **hear our prayer.**

God our Lord, you desire that we should seek your Kingdom of harmony and joy:
- open our eyes to see each other as human beings, created in your image, but with a rich diversity of gifts …
- give us respect for one another and a determination to work through our differences and prejudices …
- guide our Queen and the leaders of all countries and communities to serve people for the common good …

Lord God, **hear our prayer.**

God our Saviour, you know our weakness and forgive our sins, we place within your loving care all who suffer from drought and disaster, war and oppression, poverty and loneliness, disease and pain …
Bless those who come to their aid, offering support, healing and hope.
Saviour God, **hear our prayer.**

We give thanks for those whose memory we treasure …
Grant us, with them, (with N.) and all the saints, the joy of eternal life in Christ, our Lord. **Amen.**

THE LORD'S PRAYER

(A HYMN may be sung)

CONCLUDING PRAYER

Bless to us, O God,
The sun that is above us,
The earth that is beneath us,
The friends who are around us,
Your image deep within us,
The rest which is before us. **Amen.**
(Celtic traditional prayer)

(The BLESSING or the GRACE is said)

THE SUNDAY NEXT BEFORE LENT
'The Transfiguration of Jesus'

> Today we recall a turning point in Jesus' life. In a startling disclosure on the mountain, the disciples were shown that he was not only the one who fulfilled the old religion of Israel (represented by Moses and Elijah) but also the beloved Son of God who would bring in the new. Later Jesus explained that first there was suffering to come. On Ash Wednesday we join him on 'the way of the cross'.

The Gathering

THE GREETING
The Lord of glory be with you.
The Lord bless you.

(A HYMN may be sung)

The Lord is King.
Let the peoples tremble!

He sits enthroned upon the cherubim.
Let the earth quake!

Let them praise your great and awesome Name.
Holy is he!

Moses and Aaron were among his priests:
They cried to the Lord and he answered them.

Extol the Lord our God, and worship at his holy mountain.
For the Lord our God is holy.
(Ps. 99:1-3, 6, 9)

PRAYER
Almighty God,
to whom all hearts are open,
all desires known, and from whom no secrets are hidden:
cleanse the thoughts of our hearts
by the inspiration of your Holy Spirit,
that we may perfectly love you,
and worthily magnify your holy name;
through Christ our Lord. **Amen.**

(SONGS may be sung)

* * * * *

PENITENCE
'A cloud overshadowed them, and from the cloud there came a voice, "This is my Son, the Beloved; listen to him!"' *(Mark 9:7)*

Father, we confess that we have not paid heed to the teaching of your Son Jesus Christ. Too often we have followed our own selfish desires and neglected the needs of others. *(silence)*

Let us confess our sins in penitence and faith.
Almighty God, our heavenly Father,
we have sinned against you
and against our neighbour
in thought and word and deed,
through negligence, through weakness,
through our own deliberate fault.
We are truly sorry
and repent of all our sins.
For the sake of your Son Jesus Christ,
who died for us,
forgive us all that is past and grant that
we may serve you in newness of life;
to the glory of your name. **Amen.**

May Almighty God have mercy on *us*,
forgive *us our* sins,
and bring *us* to everlasting life,
through Jesus Christ our Lord. **Amen**.

(The GLORIA, the VENITE, a SONG or RESPONSES may be used)

THE COLLECT OF THE DAY
Let us pray ... *(silent prayer)*

Almighty Father, whose Son was revealed in majesty before he suffered death upon the cross: give us grace to perceive his glory, that we may be strengthened to suffer with him and be changed into his likeness, from glory to glory,
who is alive and reigns with you, in the unity of the Holy Spirit, one God, now and for ever. **Amen.**

The Liturgy of the Word

THE SCRIPTURE READING(S)

(After the reading)
This is the Word of the Lord.
Thanks be to God.

PSALM/HYMN or SCRIPTURAL SONG

THE GOSPEL

Hear the Gospel of our Lord Jesus Christ according to N.
Glory to you, O Lord.

(After the reading)
This is the Gospel of the Lord.
Praise to you, O Christ.

THE SERMON

AFFIRMATION OF FAITH

I believe in God, the Father almighty, creator of heaven and earth.
I believe in Jesus Christ, his only Son, our Lord,
who was conceived by the Holy Spirit, born of the Virgin Mary,
suffered under Pontius Pilate, was crucified, died and was buried; he descended to the dead.
On the third day he rose again; he ascended into heaven,
he is seated at the right hand of the Father
and he will come to judge the living and the dead.

I believe in the Holy Spirit, the holy catholic Church, the communion of saints, the forgiveness of sins, the resurrection of the body, and the life everlasting. **Amen.**

(The Apostles' Creed)

(A HYMN may be sung)

The Prayers

INTERCESSIONS

(Special thanksgivings and prayers …)

Our Father in heaven, we bring to you the needs of the world, knowing that you hear our prayers and work out your good purposes through those who believe.

We pray for the Church in this diocese: for our bishops, clergy and lay ministers … Send more people to serve Christ in his Church, here and overseas, both lay and ordained, part-time and full-time … Bless all who are in training for ministry … Grant us your Holy Spirit that together we may walk in the way of Christ.
Lord of glory, **shine upon us.**

We pray for our Queen and country, and for all nations and their leaders … strengthen them, and us, to work for justice, search for peace and overcome evil with good.
Lord of glory, **shine upon us.**

We pray for families to be loving and stable, and our community to be caring and vibrant … Help those in difficulty to find the right way through their problems.
Lord of glory, **shine upon us.**

We pray for those suffering pain or ill-health … for the mentally or emotionally distressed … Bring strength, healing and encouragement through those who care for them …
Lord of glory, **shine upon us.**

We give thanks for those who have died … Grant us with them the joy of eternal life in Christ.
Lord of glory, **shine upon us.**

Father, we remember your many blessings, given to us each day. We ask for grace to become more like your Son, Jesus Christ our Lord. **Amen.**

THE LORD'S PRAYER

(A HYMN may be sung)

CONCLUDING PRAYER

Grant, Lord, that we may hold to you without parting, worship without wearying, serve you without failing; faithfully seek you, happily find you, and for ever possess you, the only God, blessed now and always. **Amen.**

(St Anselm)

(THE BLESSING or THE GRACE is said)

THE FIRST SUNDAY OF LENT
'Christ triumphs over temptation'

> Lent (the 'lengthening' of the days) is an old English word meaning Spring. In earliest times it was observed by those who were preparing for their Baptism at Easter. Later the 40 days of Lent were identified with the 40 days when Jesus was tested in the wilderness. It is an opportunity for Christians humbly to re-examine their lives and through prayer, study and self-denial, to renew their love for God.

The Gathering

THE GREETING
The grace and mercy of our Lord Jesus Christ be with you.
And also with you.

(A HYMN may be sung)

Happy are those whose transgression is forgiven,
whose sin is covered.

Happy are those to whom the Lord imputes no iniquity
and in whose spirit there is no deceit.

While I kept silence, my body wasted away through my groaning all day long.
Then I acknowledged my sin to you,
and I did not hide my iniquity.

I said, 'I will confess my transgressions to the Lord,'
and you forgave the guilt of my sin.
(Ps. 32:1-3, 5)

PRAYER
Lord God, as we begin our journey through Lent, give us the desire to seek first your Kingdom,
the honesty to admit our failings,
and the humility to receive your forgiveness, through Jesus Christ our Lord. **Amen.**

(SONGS may be sung)

* * * * *

PENITENCE
Hear the commandments which God has given to his people, and examine your hearts.
(The following Response may be said or sung between the Commandments: **Amen. Lord, have mercy.***)*

I am the Lord your God:
you shall have no other gods but me …
You shall not make for yourself any idol …
You shall not dishonour the name of the Lord your God …
Remember the Sabbath and keep it holy …
Honour your father and your mother …
You shall not commit murder …
You shall not commit adultery …
You shall not steal …
You shall not bear false witness against your neighbour …
You shall not covet anything which belongs to your neighbour.
Amen. Lord, have mercy upon us and write all these your laws in our hearts.

In a moment of honest reflection,
let us confess to God our failure to keep these commandments …

May Almighty God have mercy on *us*,
forgive *us our* sins,
and bring *us* to everlasting life,
through Jesus Christ our Lord. **Amen**.

(The KYRIES, the VENITE, a SONG or RESPONSES may be used)

THE COLLECT OF THE DAY
Let us pray… *(silent prayer)*
Almighty God, whose Son Jesus Christ fasted forty days in the wilderness, and was tempted as we are, yet without sin: give us grace to discipline ourselves in obedience to your Spirit, and, as you know our weakness, so may we know your power to save; through Jesus Christ your Son our Lord, who is alive and reigns with you, in the unity of the Holy Spirit, one God, now and for ever.
Amen.

The Liturgy of the Word

THE SCRIPTURE READING(S)

(After the reading)
This is the Word of the Lord.
Thanks be to God.

PSALM, HYMN or SCRIPTURAL SONG

THE GOSPEL

Hear the Gospel of our Lord Jesus Christ according to N.
Glory to you, O Lord.

(After the reading)
This is the Gospel of the Lord.
Praise to you, O Christ.

THE SERMON

AFFIRMATION OF FAITH

Let us declare our faith in God:

Do you believe and trust in God the Father,
source of all being and life, the one for whom we exist?
We believe and trust in him.

Do you believe and trust in God the Son,
who took our human nature,
died for us and rose again?
We believe and trust in him.

Do you believe and trust in God the Holy Spirit, who gives life to the people of God and makes Christ known in the world?
We believe and trust in him.

This is the faith of the Church.
This is our faith.
We believe and trust in one God,
Father, Son and Holy Spirit.   Amen.

(A HYMN may be sung)

The Prayers

INTERCESSIONS

(Special thanksgivings and prayers …)

Lord Jesus, in the wilderness you refused to turn stones into bread when you were hungry because, for you, nourishment of the spirit was as important as feeding of the body. May our love for God be nourished through learning from his Word …
Lord, in your mercy,   **hear our prayer.**

Lord Jesus, you refused to throw yourself down from the top of the Temple in a reckless act of self-promotion. Help us to learn to take the lower place, to serve others, and to put all our trust in you. Guide our bishops, N., all church leaders and ministers to be examples of faithfulness, holiness and humility …
Lord, in your mercy,   **hear our prayer.**

Lord Jesus, you refused to take political power because it would have served the devil's plans. Guide all who have authority today, especially our Queen, and the leaders of all nations … Give them wisdom in their decisions, integrity of life, and dedication to work for the good of all people.
Lord, in your mercy,   **hear our prayer.**

Lord Jesus, in the wilderness you faced loneliness, physical distress and temptation. Give us the wisdom and strength to resist the lure of the selfish way out of our difficulties.
Bring healing and encouragement to those who are in trouble, sorrow, need, sickness or any other adversity …
Lord, in your mercy,   **hear our prayer.**

Lord Jesus, we remember with thanksgiving those who have died … Grant us with them, and all the saints, the joy of eternal life with you.   **Amen.**

THE LORD'S PRAYER

(A HYMN may be sung)

CONCLUDING PRAYER

Lord God, you have taught that all we have comes from you: teach us also to be faithful stewards of our time, our talents, and our possessions, that they may be generously and effectively used in the service of your Kingdom; through Jesus Christ our Lord.   Amen.

(THE BLESSING or THE GRACE is said)

THE SECOND SUNDAY OF LENT
'Return to the way of righteousness'

Today's Collect prays that we may 'return to the way of righteousness'. During Lent we are encouraged to examine our lives in the light of God's commandments, and of Christ's example, so that we realize the 'errors' that have led us astray. Then, assured of Christ's forgiveness and fellowship, we can return to the right way and 'follow all such things as are agreeable' to it.

The Gathering

THE GREETING
The grace and mercy of our Lord Jesus Christ be with you.
And also with you.

(A HYMN may be sung)

Make me to know your ways, O Lord;
teach me your paths.

Lead me in your truth, and teach me,
***for you are the God of my salvation;
for you I wait all day long.***

Do not remember the sins of my youth or my transgressions;
***according to your steadfast love
remember me, for your goodness' sake,
O Lord!*** *(Ps. 25:4-5, 7)*

PRAYER
***Almighty God, to whom
all hearts are open, all desires known,
and from whom no secrets are hidden:
cleanse the thoughts of our hearts
by the inspiration of your Holy Spirit,
that we may perfectly love you,
and worthily magnify your Holy name;
through Christ our Lord. Amen.***

(SONGS may be sung)

* * * * *

PENITENCE
Hear the commandments which God has given to his people, and examine your hearts.
*(This Response may be said or sung between the Commandments: **Amen. Lord, have mercy.**)*
I am the Lord your God:
You shall have no other gods but me …
You shall not make for yourself any idol …
You shall not dishonour the name of the Lord your God …
Remember the Sabbath and keep it holy …
Honour your father and mother …
You shall not commit murder …
You shall not commit adultery …
You shall not steal …
You shall not bear false witness against your neighbour …
You shall not covet anything which belongs to your neighbour …
***Amen. Lord, have mercy upon us and
write all these your laws in our hearts.***

In a moment of honest reflection, let us confess to God our failure to keep these commandments …

May Almighty God, who sent his Son
into the world to save sinners,
bring *us* his pardon and peace,
now and for ever. **Amen.**

(The KYRIES, the VENITE, a SONG or RESPONSES may be used)

THE COLLECT OF THE DAY
Let us pray …   *(silent prayer)*

Almighty God,
you show to those who are in error the light of your truth, that they may return to the way of righteousness:
grant to all those who are admitted into the fellowship of Christ's religion, that they may reject those things that are contrary to their profession, and follow all such things as are agreeable to the same;
through our Lord Jesus Christ, who is alive and reigns with you, in the unity of the Holy Spirit, one God, now and for ever. **Amen.**

The Liturgy of the Word

THE SCRIPTURE READING(S)

(After the reading)
This is the Word of the Lord.
Thanks be to God.

PSALM/HYMN or SCRIPTURAL SONG

THE GOSPEL
Hear the Gospel of our Lord Jesus Christ according to N.
Glory to you, O Lord.

(After the reading)
This is the Gospel of the Lord.
Praise to you, O Christ.

THE SERMON

AFFIRMATION OF FAITH
Let us declare our faith in God:

Do you believe and trust in God the Father, source of all being and life, the one for whom we exist?
We believe and trust in him.

Do you believe and trust in God the Son, who took our human nature, died for us and rose again?
We believe and trust in him.

Do you believe and trust in God the Holy Spirit, who gives life to the people of God and makes Christ known in the world?
We believe and trust in him.

This is the faith of the Church.
This is our faith.
We believe and trust in one God, Father, Son and Holy Spirit. Amen.

(A HYMN may be sung)

The Prayers

INTERCESSIONS
(Special thanksgivings and prayers …)

God the Father, **have mercy on us.**
God the Son, **have mercy on us.**
God the Holy Spirit, **have mercy on us.**
Holy, blessed, and glorious Trinity, **have mercy on us.**

From all evil and mischief; from pride, vanity, and hypocrisy; from envy, hatred, and malice; and from all evil intent,
Good Lord, deliver us.

Enlighten N. our bishop and all who minister with knowledge and understanding that by their teaching and their lives they may proclaim your Word.
R: Hear us, good Lord.

Give your people grace to hear and receive your Word and to bring forth the fruit of the Spirit. **R:**

Strengthen those who stand, comfort and help the faint-hearted, raise up the fallen; and finally beat down Satan under our feet. **R:**

Guide the leaders of the nations into the ways of peace and justice. **R:**

Help and comfort the lonely, the bereaved, and the oppressed. **R: Lord, have mercy.**

Heal the sick in body and mind, and provide for the homeless, the hungry and the destitute. **R:**

Show your pity on prisoners and refugees, and all who are in trouble. **R:**

Hear us as we remember those who have died in the peace of Christ, both those who have confessed the faith and those whose faith is known to you alone, and grant us with them a share in your eternal Kingdom. **R:**

Give us true repentance; forgive us our sins of negligence and ignorance and our deliberate sins; and grant us the grace of your Holy Spirit to amend our lives according to your holy Word.
Holy God, holy and strong, holy and immortal, have mercy on us. Amen.
(The Litany)

THE LORD'S PRAYER

(A HYMN may be sung)

CONCLUDING PRAYER
Lord, help us fight valiantly as disciples of Christ against sin, the world and the devil, and remain faithful to Christ to the end of our lives. Amen.

(The BLESSING or the GRACE is said)

THE THIRD SUNDAY OF LENT
'Walking in the way of the cross'

> Jesus Christ came to seek lost human beings, and bring them back into a right relationship with God. But it cost him dearly – his death on the cross. He calls his followers now to journey together with him 'in the way of the cross'. That means making sacrifices in the service of God and neighbour, and finding it, in the words of today's Collect, to be 'the way of life and peace'.

The Gathering

THE GREETING
Grace, mercy and peace from God our Father and the Lord Jesus Christ be with you.
And also with you.

(A HYMN may be sung)

Create in me a clean heart, O God,
and put a new and right spirit within me.

Do not cast me away from your presence,
and do not take your holy spirit from me.

Restore to me the joy of your salvation,
and sustain in me a willing spirit.

O Lord, open my lips,
and my mouth will declare your praise.
(from Isa. 51)

PRAYER
Almighty God, to whom all hearts are open, all desires known and from whom no secrets are hidden:
cleanse the thoughts of our hearts by the inspiration of your Holy Spirit, that we may perfectly love you, and worthily magnify your Holy name; through Christ our Lord. **Amen.**

(SONGS may be sung)

* * * * *

PENITENCE
Jesus' Summary of the Law
(Mark 12:29-31)
The first commandment is:
'You shall love the Lord your God with all your heart, and with all your soul, and with all your mind, and with all your strength.'

The second is this:
'You shall love your neighbour as yourself.'

There is no other commandment greater than these.
Amen. Lord have mercy.

Let us confess to God our failure to keep his commandments:
Most merciful God,
Father of our Lord Jesus Christ,
we confess that we have sinned
in thought, word and deed.
We have not loved you with our whole heart. We have not loved our neighbours as ourselves.
In your mercy forgive what we have been, help us to amend what we are, and direct what we shall be;
that we may do justly, love mercy, and walk humbly with you, our God.
Amen.

May Almighty God have mercy on *us*,
forgive *us* our sins,
and bring *us* to everlasting life,
through Jesus Christ our Lord. **Amen.**

(The KYRIES, the VENITE, or RESPONSES may be used)

THE COLLECT OF THE DAY
Let us pray … *(silent prayer)*

Almighty God, whose most dear Son went not up to joy but first he suffered pain, and entered not into glory before he was crucified: mercifully grant that we, walking in the way of the cross, may find it none other than the way of life and peace;
through Jesus Christ your Son our Lord, who is alive and reigns with you, in the unity of the Holy Spirit, one God, now and for ever.
Amen.

The Liturgy of the Word

THE SCRIPTURE READING(S)
(After the reading)
This is the Word of the Lord.
Thanks be to God.

PSALM/HYMN or SCRIPTURAL SONG

THE GOSPEL
Hear the Gospel of our Lord Jesus Christ according to N.
Glory to you, O Lord.

(After the reading)
This is the Gospel of the Lord.
Praise to you, O Christ.

THE SERMON

AFFIRMATION OF FAITH
Let us affirm our faith in God:
I believe in God, the Father almighty, creator of heaven and earth.
I believe in Jesus Christ, his only Son, our Lord,
who was conceived by the Holy Spirit, born of the Virgin Mary,
suffered under Pontius Pilate,
was crucified, died and was buried;
he descended to the dead.
On the third day he rose again;
he ascended into heaven,
he is seated at the right hand of the Father and he will come to judge the living and the dead.

I believe in the Holy Spirit,
the holy catholic Church,
the communion of saints,
the forgiveness of sins,
the resurrection of the body,
and the life everlasting. Amen.
(The Apostles' Creed)

(A HYMN may be sung)

The Prayers

INTERCESSIONS
(Special thanksgivings and prayers ...)

We bring to you, Father God, the needs of all people, for whose salvation you sent your Son Jesus Christ:

We pray for our Queen and government, and the leaders of the nations ... We think of people divided by national enmity, religious intolerance, or racial prejudice ...
Lord Jesus, where there is hatred,
let me sow love.

We pray for husbands and wives, parents and children, employers and employees ... We think of families, communities and work places where relationships have broken down ...
Lord Jesus, where there is injury,
let me sow pardon.

We pray for bishop N., for all who teach the Christian faith, and for the life of our church ... We think of those whose faith is being sorely tested ...
Lord Jesus, where there is doubt,
let me sow faith.

We remember with thanksgiving those who have died ... We think of those who are overshadowed by loss or loneliness ... We pray for all in need ... We pray for their families and friends, doctors, nurses and carers.
Lord Jesus, where there is despair,
let me give hope.

We think of ourselves, our self-centredness, our faltering attempts to serve you ...
Lord Jesus,
make us channels of your peace and witnesses of your Kingdom. Amen.

THE LORD'S PRAYER

(A HYMN may be sung)

CONCLUDING PRAYER
Teach us good Lord,
to serve thee as thou deservest;
to give and not to count the cost,
to fight and not to heed the wounds,
to toil and not to seek for rest,
to labour and not to seek reward,
save that of knowing
that we do thy will. **Amen.**
(Ignatius Loyola)

(The BLESSING or the GRACE is said)

MOTHERING SUNDAY
THE FOURTH SUNDAY OF LENT

Two old customs lie behind Mothering Sunday: young people who worked away from home were allowed to visit their mothers on this day, often presenting her with a bunch of flowers; also people were encouraged to worship in their 'Mother' Church – perhaps the Cathedral – and to celebrate by eating simnel cakes. Midway through Lent, this Sunday – also called 'Refreshment Sunday' – allows some relaxation of Lenten discipline.

The Gathering

THE GREETING
Grace and peace to you from God our Father and the Lord Jesus Christ. **Amen.**
And also with you.

(A HYMN may be sung)

THANKSGIVING
Lord God, our heavenly Father: we give thanks for each family and home, where we belong:
For mothers, who love us whatever happens,
thank you.
For fathers, who protect us and guide us,
thank you.
For brothers and sisters, who enrich family life,
thank you.
For grandparents, who have time to listen,
thank you.
Today we celebrate all that our families mean to us. **Amen.**
(SONGS may be sung)

* * * * *

DEDICATION OF FLOWERS
God, our Father in heaven,
we will never fully know
what our mothers have done for us.
We can never fully repay them
for countless gifts of love.
But we give these flowers today
as a sign of how we love them;
through Jesus Christ our Lord. **Amen.**
(The flowers are distributed to the children who take them to their mothers).

PENITENCE
Listen to God's commandment:
'Honour your father and your mother, so that your days may be long.' *(Exod. 20:12)*

Today, we remember how we often fail to give enough respect or attention to those we love …

Let us confess our sins to God:
Almighty God, our heavenly Father,
we have sinned against you,
and against our neighbour
in thought and word and deed,
through negligence, through weakness,
through our own deliberate fault.
We are truly sorry
and repent of all our sins.
For the sake of your Son Jesus Christ,
who died for us,
forgive us all that is past;
and grant that we may serve you
in newness of life
to the glory of your name. **Amen.**

May Almighty God have mercy on *us*,
forgive *us our* sins,
and bring *us* to everlasting life,
through Jesus Christ our Lord. **Amen.**

(The KYRIES, the VENITE, a SONG or RESPONSES may be used)

THE COLLECT OF THE DAY
Let us pray … *(silent prayer)*
God of compassion, whose Son Jesus Christ, the child of Mary, shared the life of a home in Nazareth, and on the cross drew the whole human family to himself:
strengthen us in our daily living that in joy and in sorrow we may know the power of your presence to bind together and to heal;
through Jesus Christ your Son our Lord, who is alive and reigns with you, in the unity of the Holy Spirit, one God, now and for ever. **Amen.**

The Liturgy of the Word

THE SCRIPTURE READING(S)

(After the reading)
This is the Word of the Lord.
Thanks be to God.

PSALM/SCRIPTURAL SONG or HYMN

THE GOSPEL
Hear the Gospel of our Lord Jesus Christ according to N.
Glory to you, O lord.

(After the reading)
This is the Gospel of the Lord.
Praise to you, O Christ.

THE SERMON

AFFIRMATION OF FAITH
Let us declare our faith in God:

**We believe in God the Father,
from whom every family
in heaven and on earth is named.**

**We believe in God the Son,
who lives in our hearts through faith,
and fills us with his love.**

**We believe in God the Holy Spirit,
who strengthens us
with power from on high.**

**We believe in one God;
Father, Son and Holy Spirit.   Amen.**
(from Eph. 3)

(A HYMN may be sung)

The Prayers

INTERCESSIONS

A Mother's Prayer
When parents brought their children to Jesus, he embraced and blessed them; Heavenly Father, we too bring children to you for your blessing. Help them know that they, and we, are always held safe in your strong but tender care.
Lord, in your mercy, ***hear our prayer.***

Jesus knew that growing up is difficult. Help us to affirm children's strengths and listen to their worries ...
Lord, in your mercy, ***hear our prayer.***

Jesus knew the security of a strong and loving home. Help us to make our children feel loved, disciplined and safe ...
Lord, in your mercy, ***hear our prayer.***

Jesus knew that every family comes under strain at times. Give us patience and a forgiving heart if relationships break down ...
Lord, in your mercy, ***hear our prayer.***

Jesus knew that sometimes parents feel they have failed. Help us to learn from our mistakes and look for fresh beginnings ...
Lord, in your mercy, ***hear our prayer.***

Jesus knew the fun of childhood. Help us to enjoy time with our children, that their vitality may touch all our lives with laughter.
Lord, in your mercy, ***hear our prayer.***

A Prayer for all families in need
O Lord our God, we pray:
for mothers who struggle to bring up children on their own ...
Merciful Lord, ***help them in their need.***

For fathers who have to work long hours away from home ...
Merciful Lord, ***help them in their need.***

For children who are disabled or abused ...
Merciful Lord, ***help them in their need.***

For all parents who have lost a child ...
Merciful Lord, ***help them in their need.***

Bless all who work with families that are poor, homeless or unable to cope ...
Hear our prayers for Christ's sake.   ***Amen.***

THE LORD'S PRAYER

(A HYMN may be sung)

CONCLUDING PRAYER
O God, as we have been blessed by a mother's love, so may we know more of your love, through Jesus Christ our Lord.   ***Amen.***

(THE BLESSING or THE GRACE is said)

THE FIFTH SUNDAY OF LENT
'Faith in him who suffered on the cross'

This 'Passion Sunday' marks the beginning of the two weeks of Passiontide (Latin *passio* – suffering) leading up to Easter. The Church commemorates the sufferings of our Lord during the last days of his earthly life. In some churches crosses, pictures and statues are veiled to emphasize the solemnity and sadness of this time.

The Gathering

THE GREETING
The grace and mercy of our Lord Jesus Christ be with you.
And also with you.

(A HYMN may be sung)

The prophet Isaiah wrote of God's servant:
He was despised and rejected by others;
a man of suffering and acquainted with infirmity.

He was wounded for our transgressions,
crushed for our iniquities;

Upon him was the punishment that made us whole,
and by his bruises we are healed.
(Isa. 53:3, 5)

PRAYER
Saviour of the world,
by your agony and trial;
by your cross and passion,
and by your precious death and burial,
Good Lord, deliver us. *Amen.*

(SONGS may be sung)
* * * * *

PENITENCE
Christ himself bore our sins in his body on the cross, so that, free from sins, we might live for righteousness. By his wounds you have been healed. *(1 Pet. 2:24)*

Calling to mind the heavy cost of human sin, and the price Jesus paid to forgive it, we confess our sins in confidence that we will be forgiven …

Almighty and most merciful Father,
we have wandered and strayed from
your ways like lost sheep.
We have followed too much the devices
and desires of our own hearts. We have
offended against your holy laws.
We have left undone those things that we
ought to have done;
and we have done those things
that we ought not to have done
and there is no health in us.
But you, O Lord,
have mercy upon us in our need.
Spare those who confess their faults.
Restore those who are penitent,
according to your promises declared to
mankind in Christ Jesus our Lord.
And grant, O most merciful Father,
for his sake, that we may live a
disciplined, righteous and godly life,
to the glory of your holy name. **Amen.**

May Almighty God have mercy on *us*,
forgive *us* our sins,
and bring *us* to everlasting life,
through Jesus Christ our Lord. **Amen**.

(The KYRIES, the VENITE, a SONG or RESPONSES may be used)

THE COLLECT OF THE DAY
Let us pray … *(silent prayer)*

Most merciful God, who by the death and resurrection of your Son Jesus Christ delivered and saved the world: grant that by faith in him who suffered on the cross we may triumph in the power of his victory; through Jesus Christ your Son our Lord, who is alive and reigns with you, in the unity of the Holy Spirit, one God, now and for ever. **Amen**.

The Liturgy of the Word

THE SCRIPTURE READING(S)

(After the reading)
This is the Word of the Lord.
Thanks be to God.

PSALM/SCRIPTURAL SONG or HYMN

THE GOSPEL
Hear the Gospel of our Lord Jesus Christ according to N.
Glory to you, O Lord.

(After the reading)
This is the Gospel of the Lord.
Praise to you, O Christ.

THE SERMON

AFFIRMATION OF FAITH
Let us affirm our faith in God:

Do you believe and trust in God the Father, source of all being and life, the one for whom we exist?
We believe and trust in him.

Do you believe and trust in God the Son, who took our human nature, died for us and rose again?
We believe and trust in him.

Do you believe and trust in God the Holy Spirit, who gives life to the people of God and makes Christ known in the world?
We believe and trust in him.

This is the faith of the Church.
This is our faith.
We believe and trust in one God,
Father, Son and Holy Spirit.   Amen.

(A HYMN may be sung)

The Prayers

INTERCESSIONS
(Special thanksgivings and prayers …)

Remembering the trials endured by Jesus Christ, we pray for all who suffer today:

Christ, born in a shelter for animals,
give hope to the homeless today.

Christ, who fled from Herod's brutal power,
guide our Queen and all rulers
in the paths of peace.

Christ, who fasted in the wilderness,
give bread to the hungry.

Christ, who resisted temptation,
grant us strength to stand against evil.

Christ, who gave up comfort and security to do God's will,
lead us to seek God's Kingdom first.

Christ, who, in the Garden, wrestled with doubt and fear,
bring the lost out of darkness and
confusion into your light.

Christ, who was condemned and tortured for crimes he never committed,
bring justice to all who are unfairly treated.

Christ, who felt pain, loneliness and humiliation as he hung on the cross,
grant healing and hope to sick and suffering people.

Christ, buried in a borrowed tomb, we remember those who have died …
grant us, with them, a share in life eternal.
Amen.

THE LORD'S PRAYER

(A HYMN may be sung)

CONCLUDING PRAYER
Lord Jesus Christ, we thank you for all the benefits you have won for us, for all the pains and insults you have borne for us. Most merciful redeemer, friend and brother,
may we know you more clearly,
love you more dearly, and follow you
more nearly, day by day.   Amen.

(THE BLESSING or THE GRACE is said)

PALM SUNDAY
'Follow the steps of Christ's patience and humility'

Holy Week recalls the last momentous week in Jesus' life: **Palm Sunday** – his ride into Jerusalem on a donkey; **Monday to Wednesday** – the cleansing of the Temple of corrupt traders, the debates with religious leaders, the anointing of his body by a woman, the plotting of his death by Judas; **Maundy Thursday** – the washing of the disciples' feet, and the Last Supper; **Good Friday** – his arrest, trial, crucifixion and burial.

The Gathering
(The people gather holding palm crosses or branches)

LITURGY OF THE PALMS
Hosanna to the Son of David!
Blessed is the one who comes in the name of the Lord! Hosanna in the highest heaven!
(Matt. 21:9)

The Lord be with you.   **And also with you.**

Friends in Christ, today we draw near to the end of our journey through Lent. During the past forty days we have been encouraged to re-examine our lives and, through disciplined prayer, Bible study and self-denial, to renew our discipleship of Christ. We have endeavoured to follow his Way, the path of sacrifice and service, and to prepare ourselves for the celebration of his resurrection.

We are gathered here to remember the day when Jesus entered his own city one last time to challenge its leaders with the message of God's unconditional love. We know that the message was rejected, and its bearer handed over to torture and death.

Let us, in union with our fellow pilgrims throughout the world, follow him now, moved by his sufferings and obedient to his call.

(The people hold up their palms and branches)

God our Father, whose Son Jesus Christ entered Jerusalem to the cheers of palm-waving crowds, let these palms and branches be a witness to his sacrifice, and a token of our faith in him, who gave his life for the world's salvation, and now lives and reigns with you and the Holy Spirit, one God for ever.   **Amen.**

Gospel Reading: He enters the city.

(A HYMN may be sung; the people may process through the church)

PENITENCE
On Palm Sunday, the crowds hailed Jesus as King; on Good Friday they shouted for him to die. Confessing that our faith is often shallow, we ask forgiveness for our sins.

Lord Jesus, you come to us in peace, but we find it hard to make peace with others.
Lord, have mercy,   **Lord, have mercy.**

You come to us in humility, but we like to be the centre of attention.
Christ, have mercy,   **Christ, have mercy.**

You come to us offering forgiveness, but we blame others for our failures.
Lord, have mercy,   **Lord, have mercy.**

You come to us as the servant King, but we prefer to serve our own interests.
Lord, forgive us and help us.

May almighty God, who sent his Son
into the world to save sinners,
bring *us* his pardon and peace,
now and for ever.

(The KYRIES, the VENITE, a SONG or RESPONSES may be used)

THE COLLECT OF THE DAY
Let us pray ...   *(silent prayer)*
Almighty and everlasting God,
who in your tender love towards the human race sent your Son our Saviour Jesus Christ, to take upon him our flesh and to suffer death upon the cross: grant that we may follow the example of his patience and humility, and also be made partakers of his resurrection; through Jesus Christ your Son our Lord, who is alive and reigns with you, in the unity of the Holy Spirit, one God, now and for ever.   **Amen.**

The Liturgy of the Word

THE SCRIPTURE READING(S)

(After the reading)
This is the Word of the Lord.
Thanks be to God.

PSALM/HYMN or SCRIPTURAL SONG

THE GOSPEL
Hear the Gospel of our Lord Jesus Christ according to N.
Glory to you, O Lord.

(After the reading)
This is the Gospel of the Lord.
Praise to you, O Christ.

THE SERMON

AFFIRMATION OF FAITH
Let us affirm our faith in Jesus Christ, the Son of God:

*Though he was divine,
he did not cling to equality with God,
but made himself nothing.
Taking the form of a slave,
he was born in human likeness.
He humbled himself, and was obedient
to death – even the death of the cross.
Therefore God has raised him on high,
and given him the name above every
name: that at the name of Jesus
every knee should bow,
and every voice proclaim
that Jesus Christ is Lord,
to the glory of God the Father.*
(from Phil. 2:6-11)

This is the faith of the Church.
***This is our faith.
We believe and trust in one God,
Father, Son and Holy Spirit
Amen.***

(A HYMN may be sung)

The Prayers

INTERCESSIONS
(Special thanksgivings and prayers …)

We pray that the Lord Jesus, who entered Jerusalem on Palm Sunday to cleanse and save God's people, will today find us ready to follow him:

Lord, as you gave us an example of humble service, so guide our Queen and all leaders to serve their people with devotion, and bring peace between the nations …
In your mercy, **hear our prayer.**

Lord, as you sacrificed your life for the world's salvation so give strength and patience to those who make great sacrifices in their care of others …
In your mercy, **hear our prayer.**

Lord, as you cleansed the Temple, so cleanse your Church today of disunity, hypocrisy and complacency …
In your mercy, **hear our prayer.**

Lord, as you taught the people the truth about God, teach us your ways, reveal your love, and send us out with your Spirit to serve others.
In your mercy, **hear our prayer.**

Lord, be close to those who suffer … grant them healing, strength and encouragement.
In your mercy, **hear our prayer.**

Saviour of the world, by your agony and trial, by your cross and passion, and by your precious death and burial, **good Lord, deliver us.**

Remembering those who have died … grant us, with them, a share in your eternal Kingdom. **Amen.**

THE LORD'S PRAYER

(A HYMN may be sung)

CONCLUDING PRAYER
*Lord Jesus, as the crowds long ago
welcomed you with shouts of Hosanna,
we also welcome you,
not with empty praise
and shallow promises,
but with grateful hearts
that long to serve you,
day by day.* **Amen.**

(THE BLESSING or THE GRACE is said)

GOOD FRIDAY
'Jesus Christ ... given up into the hands of sinners'

Today we are called to solemn remembrance of the final sufferings of Jesus: betrayed by Judas, arrested as a criminal, deserted by his friends, tried and convicted on false charges, gratuitously tortured, brutally crucified, hastily buried in a borrowed tomb. Images, symbols and silence, as well as words and music, help us comprehend the sorrows of this day. It is called Good Friday because the suffering was not in vain.

The Gathering

THE GREETING
The Lord be with you.
The Lord bless you.

Dear Friends, we have gathered here on this most solemn of days to recall a decisive moment in the story of the world's salvation.

Through the long years of human history God has served his people in justice and compassion so that they may discover the joy of living in fellowship with one another. But deep in the heart of man self-interest and rebellion have always stirred up prejudice and hatred, envy and greed, setting each person against their neighbour.

On Good Friday, on the cross of Christ, the perfect love of one man was overwhelmed by the power of darkness. Today, we lament the suffering, not only of the Crucified One, but also of all other innocent victims of evil.

In this act of remembrance, we are invited not to stand apart and stare, but to recognize the shadows in our own lives which have lengthened those that once engulfed God's Son. May we see ourselves as participants in the drama enacted on this fateful day, and look on Christ's death as the ultimate sacrifice, offered to forgive our sins.

It began in the early hours of the morning ...
'Suddenly a crowd came, and the one called Judas ... was leading them. He approached Jesus to kiss him; but Jesus said to him: "Judas, is it with a kiss that you are betraying the Son of Man?" Then Jesus said to the chief priests, "Have you come out with swords and clubs as if I were a bandit ... But this is your hour, and the power of darkness."'
(Luke 22:47-8, 52-3)

(A HYMN may be sung)

PENITENCE
(A shortened LITANY may be used:)

God the Father,   **have mercy upon us.**
God the Son,   **have mercy upon us.**
God the Holy Spirit,   **have mercy upon us.**
Holy, blessed and glorious Trinity,
                        have mercy upon us.

From all evil and mischief; from pride, vanity and hypocrisy; from envy, hatred and malice; and from all evil intent,
R: good Lord, deliver us.

By your agony and trial;
by your cross and passion;
and by your precious death and burial. **R:**

Give us true repentance; forgive us our sins of negligence and ignorance and our deliberate sins; and grant us the grace of your Holy Spirit to amend our lives according to your holy Word.
***Holy God, holy and strong,
holy and immortal, have mercy upon us.***

May almighty God, who sent his Son into the world to save sinners, bring *us* his pardon and peace, now and for ever.   **Amen.**

THE COLLECT OF THE DAY
Let us pray ...   *(silent prayer)*

Almighty Father, look with mercy on this your family for which our Lord Jesus Christ was content to be betrayed
and given up into the hands of sinners
and to suffer death upon the cross;
who is alive and glorified with you and the Holy Spirit, one God, now and for ever.
                                    Amen.

The Liturgy of the Word

READINGS ON CHRIST'S PASSION
(These may be interspersed with hymns, songs, psalms, music or meditations)

AFFIRMATION OF FAITH
Let us affirm our faith in God:

Do you believe and trust in God the Father, source of all being and life, the one for whom we exist?
We believe and trust in him.

Do you believe and trust in God the Son, who took our human nature, died for us and rose again?
We believe and trust in him

Do you believe and trust in God the Holy Spirit, who gives life to the people of God and makes Christ known in the world?
We believe and trust in him.

This is the faith of the Church.
This is our faith.
We believe and trust in one God,
Father, Son and Holy Spirit. **Amen.**

(A HYMN may be sung)

The Prayers

INTERCESSIONS
(Based on 'the Seven Last Words' from the cross)

'Father, forgive them, for they do not know what they are doing'
Like those who crucified Jesus, we are sometimes unaware of the hurt we inflict on others. Lord, give us the desire, in all situations of conflict, to seek understanding, forgiveness and reconciliation, but never revenge. We pray for nations and communities divided by deep and ancient enmities …
Your Kingdom come, **Your will be done.**

'Today you will be with me in Paradise'
Like the penitent criminal crucified alongside Jesus, we confess we have no one to blame for our sins but ourselves. Lord, give us the humility to accept responsibility for our failings and to place our hope in you. We pray for those in prison for their crimes, and those persecuted for their beliefs …
Your Kingdom come, **Your will be done.**

'Woman, here is your son'
Like Mary, alone in her grief, we need each other's support in the trials and sorrows of life. Lord, give us compassion to care for for those around us, and for those who need us. We pray for our families … We pray for the Church family, and for all who minister …
Your Kingdom come, **Your will be done.**

'I am thirsty'
Like the bystanders who did little to assuage Jesus' thirst, we too feel helpless in the face of unending human need. Inspire us, Lord, to light the flame of love, and fan it by your Spirit to embrace the world …
Your Kingdom come, **Your will be done.**

'My God, my God, why have you forsaken me?'
In those moments when catastrophe strikes and hope itself deserts us, make us know, Lord, that nothing can frustrate your good purposes nor separate us from your love. We pray for all who are overwhelmed by worry, loss or tragedy …
Your Kingdom come, **Your will be done.**

'Father, into your hands I commend my spirit'
When earthly life ends help us, Lord, to let go of worldly supports and entrust ourselves wholly to your fatherly care. We pray for the dying, and for those who sit with them …
Your Kingdom come, **Your will be done.**

'It is finished'
In self-giving and vulnerability, Lord, you fulfil your work of salvation. Help us to know, and bear witness to, the victory over evil and death by which your Kingdom comes, through Jesus Christ our Lord. **Amen.**

THE LORD'S PRAYER

(A HYMN may be sung)

CONCLUDING PRAYER
We adore you, O Christ, and we bless you, because by your holy cross you have redeemed the world. **Amen.**

(The people depart in silence)

EASTER DAY
'Christ is risen Alleluia!'

The first Easter was the day that changed everything. The rule of sin and death – the 'old order' mentioned in the Collect – which undermines all human endeavour, was overcome by the death and resurrection of Christ. By faith in him we are freed from that 'old order', to share in a new life. Now we know we are the beloved children of the Father in heaven, called to bear witness to his Kingdom on earth.

The Gathering

THE GREETING
Alleluia, Christ is risen.
He is risen indeed, Alleluia!

(A HYMN may be sung)

This is the day that dispels the darkness.
Alleluia! Christ is risen.
This is the day that proclaims God's love.
Alleluia! Christ is risen.
This is the day that celebrates life.
Alleluia! Christ is risen.
This is the day that reveals what is good.
Alleluia! Christ is risen.
This is the day that starts a journey.
Alleluia! Christ is risen.
This is the day that the Lord has made.
Let us rejoice and be glad in it.

PRAYER
Lord Jesus Christ,
as we celebrate your victory
over all the powers of darkness, evil and
death, we pray that we will know your
strength to rise above our fears and failures,
and travel on with you in the way of love.
                                      Amen.

(SONGS may be sung)

         *   *   *   *   *

PENITENCE
Christ our Passover lamb has been
sacrificed for us. Let us therefore rejoice by
putting away all malice and evil and
confessing our sins with a sincere and true
heart ...   *(1 Cor. 5:7-8)*

Almighty God, our heavenly Father,
we have sinned against you
and against our neighbour
in thought and word and deed,
through negligence, through weakness,
through our own deliberate fault.
We are truly sorry
and repent of all our sins.
For the sake of your Son Jesus Christ,
who died for us,
forgive us all that is past and grant
that we may serve you in newness of life
to the glory of your name.   **Amen.**

Almighty God,
who forgives all who truly repent,
have mercy upon *us*,
pardon and deliver *us* from all *our* sins,
confirm and strengthen *us* in all goodness,
and keep *us* in life eternal;
through Jesus Christ our Lord.   **Amen.**

(The GLORIA, the VENITE, a SONG or RESPONSES may be used)

THE COLLECT OF THE DAY
Let us pray ...   *(silent prayer)*

Lord of all life and power, who through
the mighty resurrection of your Son
overcame the old order of sin and death to
make all things new in him:
grant that we, being dead to sin
and alive to you in Jesus Christ,
may reign with him in glory;
to whom with you and the Holy Spirit be
praise and honour, glory and might,
now and in all eternity.   **Amen.**

The Liturgy of the Word

THE SCRIPTURE READING(S)

(After the reading)
This is the Word of the Lord.
Thanks be to God.

PSALM/HYMN or EASTER ANTHEMS

THE GOSPEL
Hear the Gospel of our Lord Jesus Christ according to N.
Glory to you, O Lord.

(After the reading)
This is the Gospel of the Lord.
Praise to you, O Christ.

THE SERMON

AFFIRMATION OF FAITH

We believe in one God, the Father, the Almighty, maker of heaven and earth, of all that is, seen and unseen.

We believe in one Lord, Jesus Christ, the only Son of God, eternally begotten of the Father, God from God, Light from Light, true God from true God, begotten, not made, of one Being with the Father; through him all things were made.

For us and for our salvation he came down from heaven, was incarnate from the Holy Spirit and the Virgin Mary, and was made man.
For our sake he was crucified under Pontius Pilate; he suffered death and was buried.
On the third day he rose again in accordance with the Scriptures; he ascended into heaven and is seated at the right hand of the Father.
He will come again in glory to judge the living and the dead, and his Kingdom will have no end.

We believe in the Holy Spirit, the Lord, the giver of life, who proceeds from the Father and the Son, who with the Father and the Son is worshipped and glorified, who has spoken through the prophets.

We believe in one holy catholic and apostolic Church. We acknowledge one baptism for the forgiveness of sins. We look for the resurrection of the dead, and the life of the world to come. **Amen.**

(The Nicene Creed)

(A HYMN may be sung)

The Prayers

INTERCESSIONS
(Special thanksgivings and prayers …)

Father in heaven, today we rejoice that Christ is risen from the dead:
Believing that goodness is stronger than evil, we pray for the victims of brutality and injustice … Give them hope that good will prevail. Guide our Queen, and all leaders, to work for peace, justice and a better world.
Father, in your mercy, **hear our prayer.**

Believing that love is stronger than hate, we pray for those who are rejected or abused … Give courage to all who reach across barriers of race, religion and history to promote friendship and reconciliation. Bless all who serve our neighbourhood, enriching its common life.
Father, in your mercy, **hear our prayer.**

Believing that light is stronger than darkness, we pray for those who are ignorant of your truth, or alienated from your love … Give grace to our bishop N., to church ministers, and to us your people, that we may grow in Christ and bear witness to the new life in him.
Father, in your mercy, **hear our prayer.**

Believing that life is stronger than death, we pray for those who, like Mary Magdalene, are lost in their grief or pain ... Strengthen them with faith, that nothing, not even death, can separate them from Christ's love.
Father, in your mercy, **hear our prayers through Christ, our risen Lord. Amen.**

THE LORD'S PRAYER

(A HYMN may be sung)

CONCLUDING PRAYER
Alleluia. Christ is risen!
He is risen indeed. Alleluia! Amen.

(THE BLESSING or THE GRACE is said)

THE SECOND SUNDAY OF EASTER
'Jesus Christ ... is alive and reigns'

It has been said that Christians are 'an Easter people, and Alleluia is their song.' Why? Because the resurrection of Jesus Christ from the dead gives them the hope that, in all circumstances, however dire, God works for good. The Gospel reading for today describes encounters between the risen Christ and the disciples, in which their fears and unbelief gave way to new faith, hope and joy.

The Gathering

THE GREETING
Alleluia! Christ is risen.
He is risen indeed. Alleluia!

(A HYMN may be sung)

Blessed be the God and Father of our Lord Jesus Christ!
By his great mercy he has given us a new birth into a living hope
through the resurrection of Jesus Christ from the dead.
Through him you have come to trust in God,
who raised him from the dead and gave him glory,
so that your faith and hope are set on God.   *(1 Pet. 1:3, 21)*

PRAYER
Lord Jesus Christ,
risen from death to life in the Father's love,
raise us to share in the new life, that we may know your presence among us now,
and serve you in the power of the Spirit.
Amen.

(SONGS may be sung)

* * * * *

PENITENCE
'The doors of the house where the disciples had met were locked for fear of the Jews;
Jesus came and stood among them
and said, "Peace be with you."'   *(John 20:19)*
In this Easter season we bring our fears and failings to the risen Christ:

When we are faced with a challenge, but regress into old attitudes ...
Lord, have mercy.   **Lord, have mercy.**

When we allow past hurts to undermine our present relationships ...
Christ, have mercy.   **Christ, have mercy.**

When we face difficult times but fail to trust in your loving purposes ...
Lord, have mercy.   **Lord, have mercy.**

When we look inwards to our selfish concerns rather than outwards to a world in need ...
Christ, have mercy,   **Christ, have mercy.**

When we are agents of gloom rather than messengers of hope ...
Lord, have mercy,   **Lord, have mercy.**

May Almighty God have mercy on *us*,
forgive *us our* sins
and bring *us* to everlasting life,
through Jesus Christ our Lord.   **Amen.**

(The GLORIA, the VENITE, a SONG or RESPONSES may be used)

THE COLLECT OF THE DAY
Let us pray ...   *(silent prayer)*

Almighty Father,
you have given your only Son to die for our sins and to rise again for our justification:
grant us so to put away the leaven of malice and wickedness that we may always serve you in pureness of living and truth;
through the merits of your Son
Jesus Christ our Lord,
who is alive and reigns with you,
in the unity of the Holy Spirit,
one God, now and for ever.   **Amen.**

The Liturgy of the Word

THE SCRIPTURE READING(S)

(After the reading)
This is the Word of the Lord.
Thanks be to God.

PSALM/HYMN or EASTER ANTHEMS

THE GOSPEL
Hear the Gospel of our Lord Jesus Christ according to N.
Glory to you, O Lord.

(After the reading)
This is the Gospel of the Lord.
Praise to you, O Christ.

THE SERMON

AFFIRMATION OF FAITH
Let us declare our faith in the resurrection of our Lord Jesus Christ:

Christ died for our sins
in accordance with the Scriptures;

he was buried; he was raised to life on the third day
in accordance with the Scriptures;

afterwards he appeared to his followers,
and to all the apostles:

this we have received,
and this we believe. *(1 Cor. 15:3-7)*

This is the faith of the Church.
**This is our faith.
We believe and trust in one God,
Father, Son and Holy Spirit.   Amen.**

(A HYMN may be sung)

The Prayers

INTERCESSIONS
(Special thanksgivings and prayers ...)
Our loving Father in heaven, as we recall the change that came over the disciples when they met the risen Christ on that first Easter Day, we pray for the renewal of faith, hope and love among your people today:

We pray for our fellow human beings living in fear of persecution and violence ... Strengthen their hope that peace and justice will prevail. Guide our Queen and the leaders of the nations.
At Easter, Lord,
renew our hope in your victory over evil.

We pray for those who, like Thomas, struggle with doubts and hard questions ... Make yourself known to them through the good news that Christ is alive, and through the witness of his followers.
At Easter, Lord,
renew us by your Spirit.

We pray for those who, like the disciples, are burdened by guilt, failure or grief ... Give them a fresh awareness of Christ's love and forgiveness.
At Easter, Lord,
renew our joy in your amazing grace.

We pray for all who are sent into the world to bear witness to Christ; for bishop N., for ministers and missionaries ... Lead us by your Holy Spirit into new ways of serving you.
At Easter, Lord,
renew our commitment to your service.

We pray for those who are ill or frail ... Grant them healing and encouragement.
At Easter, Lord,
renew our trust in your fatherly care.

We remember those who have died ...
We join with all Christians in lifting our voices to proclaim the living Christ as
our Lord and our God. Amen.

THE LORD'S PRAYER

(A HYMN may be sung)

CONCLUDING PRAYER

God the Father, by whose glory Christ was raised from the dead, strengthen you to walk with him in his risen life.
Amen. Alleluia! Alleluia!

(The BLESSING or the GRACE is said)

THE THIRD SUNDAY OF EASTER
'Give us knowledge of Christ's presence with us'

> During the forty days after Easter, Jesus appeared to his disciples on different occasions and in different ways. His appearances usually took them by surprise, but filled them with joy. Often it was when he shared food with them that their eyes were really opened to his risen presence among them. May our worship today, in the words of today's Collect, 'give us such knowledge of his presence with us'.

The Gathering

THE GREETING
Alleluia! Christ is risen.
He is risen indeed. Alleluia!

(A HYMN may be sung)

Christ has been raised from the dead,
the first fruits of those who have died.

I will tell you a mystery! We will not all die,
but we will all be changed.

Where, O death, is your victory?
Where, O death is your sting?

Thanks be to God,
**who gives us the victory
through our Lord Jesus Christ.**
(from 1 Cor. 15)

PRAYER
Lord Jesus Christ,
risen from death, and among us now,
make yourself known to us in our worship,
in the teaching of your Word,
in the fellowship of your people,
and in the breaking of the bread.   **Amen.**

(SONGS may be sung)

* * * * *

PENITENCE
'The doors of the house where the disciples had met were locked for fear of the Jews; Jesus came and stood among them and said, "Peace be with you."'   *(John 20:19)*

In this Easter season we bring our fears and failings to the risen Christ.

When we are faced with a challenge but regress into old attitudes ...
Lord, have mercy.   **Lord, have mercy.**

When we allow past hurts to undermine our present relationships ...
Christ, have mercy.   **Christ, have mercy.**

When we face difficult times but fail to trust in your loving purposes ...
Lord, have mercy.   **Lord, have mercy.**

When we look inwards to our selfish concerns rather than outwards to a world in need ...
Christ, have mercy,   **Christ, have mercy.**

When we are agents of gloom rather than messengers of hope ...
Lord, have mercy,   **Lord, have mercy.**

May Almighty God have mercy on *us*,
forgive *us our* sins
and bring *us* to everlasting life,
through Jesus Christ our Lord.   **Amen.**

(The GLORIA, the VENITE, a SONG or RESPONSE may be used)

THE COLLECT OF THE DAY
Let us pray ...   *(silent prayer)*

Almighty Father,
who in your great mercy gladdened the disciples with the sight of the risen Lord:
give us such knowledge of his presence with us, that we may be strengthened and sustained by his risen life and serve you continually in righteousness and truth;
through Jesus Christ your Son our Lord,
who is alive and reigns with you,
in the unity of the Holy Spirit,
one God, now and for ever.
Amen.

The Liturgy of the Word

THE SCRIPTURE READING(S)

(After the reading)
This is the Word of the Lord.
Thanks be to God.

PSALM/HYMN or EASTER ANTHEMS

THE GOSPEL
Hear the Gospel of our Lord Jesus Christ according to N.
Glory to you, O Lord.

(After the reading)
This is the Gospel of the Lord.
Praise to you, O Christ.

THE SERMON

AFFIRMATION OF FAITH
Let us declare our faith in the resurrection of our Lord Jesus Christ:

Christ died for our sins
in accordance with the Scriptures;

he was buried; he was raised to life on the third day
in accordance with the Scriptures;

afterwards he appeared to his followers, and to all the apostles:

this we have received,
and this we believe.   (1 Cor. 15:3-7)

This is the faith of the Church.
This is our faith.
We believe and trust in one God,
Father, Son and Holy Spirit.   Amen.

(A HYMN may be sung)

The Prayers

INTERCESSIONS
(Special thanksgivings and prayers …)

Father in heaven, we pray for those who, like the two disciples on the Emmaus Road, are confused in their faith and despondent about life …
Grant that we may encourage each other on the journey of faith, and know Christ's presence as we learn from the Scriptures.
Merciful Father,   **hear us we pray.**

We pray for all who have recently discovered the reality of the risen Christ …
Strengthen the Church, bishop N., and all ministers, to nourish faith through sound teaching, spiritual worship and pastoral care.
Merciful Father,   **hear us we pray.**

We pray for those who are experiencing the horrors of war, brutal persecution, or lonely exile from their homeland …
Guide our Queen, and governments of all nations, to create the conditions for peace and justice to flourish.
Merciful Father,   **hear us we pray.**

We pray for the Church when, as the first disciples found, its efforts to evangelize seem fruitless, and numbers are low …
Inspire us to find new ways of proclaiming the gospel in today's culture.
Merciful Father,   **hear us we pray.**

We pray for church leaders when, like Simon Peter, they suffer personal failure, criticism and a loss of self-confidence …
Renew their response to Christ's call to feed his flock, and strengthen us to work together in the Church's ministry.
Merciful Father,   **hear us we pray.**

We pray for those who suffer from ill-health or cope with disability … We remember those who have died and all who mourn … Keep hope alive when the burdens of life grow heavy.
Merciful Father,   **hear us we pray,**
through Christ our Lord. Amen.

THE LORD'S PRAYER

(A HYMN may be sung)

CONCLUDING PRAYER

God the Father, by whose glory Christ was raised from the dead, strengthen you to walk with him in his risen life.
Amen. Alleluia! Alleluia!

(The BLESSING or the GRACE is said)

THE FOURTH SUNDAY OF EASTER
'Seek those things which are above'

> Like a young plant that defiantly emerges from winter's cold earth, the first Easter Day was the sure sign that a new chapter had begun in the human quest for God. The resurrection of Jesus Christ gives us hope that all may rise from spiritual darkness into a new relationship with God, 'seeking' – as today's Collect puts it – 'those things which are above' – the coming of his Kingdom on earth as in heaven.

The Gathering

THE GREETING
Alleluia! Christ is risen.
He is risen indeed. Alleluia!

(A HYMN may be sung)

Remember Jesus Christ, raised from the dead:
If we have died with him,
we will also live with him;
if we endure,
we will also reign with him;
if we deny him,
he will also deny us;
if we are faithless,
he remains faithful.

The Lord will rescue me from every evil attack and save me for his heavenly Kingdom.
To him be the glory forever and ever. Amen.   *(2 Tim. 2:8, 11-13; 4:18)*

(SONGS may be sung)

* * * * *

PENITENCE
In a moment of quiet reflection, let us honestly examine our lives, remembering where our attitudes have been wrong, where love has grown cold, where hurts have not been forgiven, or where cries for help have not been answered …

Let us confess our sins in penitence and faith, firmly resolved to keep God's commandments and to live in love and peace with all.

Most merciful God,
Father of our Lord Jesus Christ,
we confess that we have sinned
in thought, word and deed.
We have not loved you with our whole heart.
We have not loved our neighbours as ourselves.
In your mercy
forgive what we have been,
help us to amend what we are,
and direct what we shall be;
that we may do justly,
love mercy,
and walk humbly with you, our God.
                                                    Amen.

May Almighty God have mercy on *us*,
forgive *us our* sins
and bring *us* to everlasting life,
through Jesus Christ our Lord.   **Amen.**

(The GLORIA, the VENITE, a SONG or RESPONSES may be used)

THE COLLECT OF THE DAY
Let us pray …   *(silent prayer)*

Almighty God,
whose Son Jesus Christ
Is the resurrection and the life:
raise us, who trust in him,
from the death of sin
to the life of righteousness,
that we may seek those things which are above, where he reigns with you
in the unity of the Holy Spirit,
one God, now and for ever.   **Amen.**

The Liturgy of the Word

THE SCRIPTURE READING(S)

(After the reading)
This is the Word of the Lord.
Thanks be to God.

PSALM/HYMN or EASTER ANTHEMS

THE GOSPEL
Hear the Gospel of our Lord Jesus Christ according to N.
Glory to you, O Lord.

(After the reading)
This is the Gospel of the Lord.
Praise to you, O Christ.

THE SERMON

AFFIRMATION OF FAITH
Let us declare our faith in the resurrection of our Lord Jesus Christ:

*Christ died for our sins
in accordance with the Scriptures;*

*he was buried; he was raised to life on the third day
in accordance with the Scriptures;*

afterwards he appeared to his followers, and to all the apostles:

*this we have received,
and this we believe.* (1 Cor. 15:3-7)

This is the faith of the Church:
**This is our faith.
We believe and trust in one God,
Father, Son and Holy Spirit. Amen.**

(A HYMN may be sung)

The Prayers

INTERCESSIONS
(Special thanksgivings and prayers …)

Our Father in heaven, we pray for all people, in the name of your Son Jesus Christ:

We pray for the Church, for bishop N., and for all who lead, teach and minister in Christ's name … Grant that we may be nourished in our faith and understanding, and bear daily witness to Christ's love.
Lord of life, **in your mercy, hear us.**

We pray for the nations of the world and for those who take authority to serve the cause of justice and human well-being … Strengthen our Queen and the leaders of the nations with gifts of wisdom, courage and integrity, that your will may be done on earth as it is in heaven.
Lord of life, **in your mercy, hear us.**

We pray for those who are afflicted by natural disasters, or caught up in brutal conflicts …
Fill them with the resurrection hope that good will prevail, and bless all who stand with them in finding solutions to their difficulties.
Lord of life, **in your mercy, hear us.**

We pray for the people we are called to serve, in the home, the neighbourhood and at work … Help us to work hard at building good relationships, and to strive for reconciliation when they break down.
Lord of life, **in your mercy, hear us.**

We pray for all who suffer from illness, loneliness or loss … Raise them from despair to hopefulness and health.
Lord of life, **in your mercy, hear us.**

We remember with thanksgiving those who have died … Strengthen all who mourn, with the sure hope that, in Christ, their loved ones are raised to fullness of life.
Lord of life, **in your mercy, hear us.**

*Accept all these prayers
for the sake of your Son
our Saviour Jesus Christ.* Amen.

THE LORD'S PRAYER
(A HYMN may be sung)

CONCLUDING PRAYER
Alleluia! Christ is risen.
He is risen indeed. Alleluia!

(The BLESSING or the GRACE is said)

THE FIFTH SUNDAY OF EASTER
'Put into our minds good desires'

Easter celebrates the resurrection of Jesus Christ. If God raised his Son from death to life, bringing victory out of disaster, he can also renew human lives. Feelings of failure, rejection or resentment are changed into opportunities for healing, forgiveness and service. As today's Collect prays, God puts 'into our minds good desires' and helps us to 'bring them to good effect'.

The Gathering

THE GREETING
Alleluia! Christ is risen.
He is risen indeed. Alleluia.

(A HYMN may be sung)

Christ once raised from the dead dies no more:
death has no more dominion over him.

In dying he died to sin once for all:
in living he lives to God.

See yourselves therefore as dead to sin:
and alive to God in Jesus Christ our Lord.
Amen. (Rom. 6:9-11)

PRAYER
Lord Jesus Christ,
as we celebrate your victory over all the powers of darkness, evil and death, we pray that we will know your strength to rise above our fears and failures, and travel on with you in the way of love. ***Amen.***

(SONGS may be sung)

* * * * *

PENITENCE
In God's holy presence let us examine the words of our mouths, the deeds of our bodies, and the desires of our minds, confessing our sins to him …

When we are quick to criticize others, but slow to praise them …
Lord, have mercy, **Lord, have mercy.**

When we bear grudges, and find it hard to forgive …
Christ, have mercy, **Christ, have mercy.**

When we think we alone are right, and impose our views on others …
Lord, have mercy, **Lord, have mercy.**

When we let evil go unchallenged, and are afraid to speak the truth …
Christ, have mercy, **Christ, have mercy.**

When we are preoccupied with ourselves, and give little attention to others …
Lord, have mercy, **Lord, have mercy.**

When we trust in material things, more than in God's unfailing love …
Christ, have mercy, **Christ, have mercy.**

Almighty God,
who forgives all who truly repent,
have mercy upon *us,*
pardon and deliver *us* from all *our* sins,
confirm and strengthen *us* in all goodness,
and keep *us* in life eternal;
through Jesus Christ our Lord. ***Amen.***

(The GLORIA, the VENITE, a SONG or RESPONSES may be used)

THE COLLECT OF THE DAY
Let us pray … *(silent prayer)*

Almighty God,
who through your only-begotten Son Jesus Christ have overcome death and opened to us the gate of everlasting life: grant that, as by your grace going before us you put into our minds good desires, so by your continual help we may bring them to good effect;
through Jesus Christ our risen Lord,
who is alive and reigns with you,
in the unity of the Holy Spirit,
one God, now and for ever. ***Amen.***

The Liturgy of the Word

THE SCRIPTURE READING(S)

(After the reading)
This is the Word of the Lord.
Thanks be to God.

PSALM/HYMN or EASTER ANTHEMS

THE GOSPEL
Hear the Gospel of our Lord Jesus Christ according to N.
Glory to you, O Lord.

(After the reading)
This is the Gospel of the Lord.
Praise to you, O Christ.

THE SERMON

AFFIRMATION OF FAITH
Let us declare our faith in the resurrection of our Lord Jesus Christ:

Christ died for our sins
in accordance with the Scriptures;

he was buried; he was raised to life on the third day
in accordance with the Scriptures;

afterwards he appeared to his followers,
and to all the apostles:

this we have received,
and this we believe.   *(1 Cor. 15:3-7)*

This is the faith of the Church:
**This is our faith.
We believe and trust in one God,
Father, Son and Holy Spirit.   Amen.**

(A HYMN may be sung)

The Prayers

INTERCESSIONS
(Special thanksgivings and prayers …)

Father God, we pray for your holy catholic apostolic Church;
**that all may be one in Christ,
our risen Saviour.**

Grant that every member of the Church may grow in knowledge of you, and faithfully serve you;
**that your Kingdom may come
and your will be done.**

We pray for bishop N., all clergy and lay workers;
**that they may be faithful ministers
of your truth and grace.**

We pray for our Queen and all who hold authority in the nations of the world;
**that there may be justice and peace
on the earth.**

Give us grace to do your will in all that we plan and do;
that our works may bring glory to your Name.

Fill us with compassion for those who suffer from any grief, trouble or injustice;
that they may be delivered from distress.

We remember with thanksgiving those who have died … We praise you for your saints who have entered into eternal rest;
**may we also come to share in your
eternal joy.**

In a moment of silence, let us pray for those we most deeply care about …
Merciful Father,
**accept all these prayers
for the sake of your Son
our Saviour Jesus Christ.   Amen.**

THE LORD'S PRAYER

(A HYMN may be sung)

CONCLUDING PRAYER

*O gracious and holy Father, give us
     wisdom to perceive you,
     diligence to seek you,
     patience to wait for you,
     eyes to behold you,
     a heart to meditate upon you,
     and a life to proclaim you;
through the power of the Spirit of Jesus
Christ our Lord. Amen.   (St Benedict)*

(The BLESSING or the GRACE is said)

THE SIXTH SUNDAY OF EASTER
ROGATION SUNDAY

> The Sixth Sunday of Easter is sometimes also known as 'Rogation Sunday' (Latin *rogare* – to ask) when the Church prays especially for all who work in agriculture. In country areas, people traditionally process through the fields praying for God's blessing on the crops and livestock. Today the Church also anticipates the great festival (next Thursday) of our Lord's Ascension into heaven, having completed his saving work on earth.

The Gathering

THE GREETING
Alleluia! Christ is risen.
He is risen indeed. Alleluia.

(A HYMN may be sung)

The Lord is faithful in all his words,
and gracious in all his deeds.

The Lord upholds all who are falling,
and raises up all who are bowed down.

The eyes of all look to you,
and you give them their food in due season.

You open your hand,
satisfying the desire of every living thing.
(Ps. 145:13-16)

PRAYER
God of heaven and earth,
you call us to share in the care of creation
and to bring food and fruitfulness
from field and farm.
Hear our prayers on this Rogation Sunday
for all who make their living on the land,
through Jesus Christ our Lord.   **Amen.**

(SONGS may be sung)

* * * * *

PENITENCE
Hear the word of the prophet Isaiah: 'The earth dries up and withers ... the earth lies polluted under its inhabitants, for they have transgressed laws ... broken the everlasting Covenant.'   *(Isa. 24:4-5)*

Let us confess our sins against God, and mankind's abuse of his Creation:

When we demand cheap food without thought of the well-being of the growers, the farm animals or the land itself ...
Lord, have mercy.   **Lord, have mercy.**

When we fail to consider those who produce our food in difficult conditions for meagre rewards ...
Christ, have mercy.   **Christ, have mercy.**

When we forget to give thanks to God for good food and clean water ...
Lord, have mercy.   **Lord, have mercy.**

May almighty God have mercy on *us*,
forgive *us* our sins
and bring *us* to everlasting life,
through Jesus Christ our Lord.   **Amen.**

(The GLORIA, the VENITE, a SONG or RESPONSES may be used)

THE COLLECT OF THE DAY
Let us pray ...   *(silent prayer)*

God our redeemer,
you have delivered us from the power of darkness and brought us into the Kingdom of your Son:
grant, that as by his death
he has recalled us to life,
so by his continual presence in us
he may raise us to eternal joy;
through Jesus Christ your Son our Lord,
who is alive and reigns with you,
in the unity of the Holy Spirit,
one God, now and for ever.   **Amen.**

The Liturgy of the Word

THE SCRIPTURE READING(S)

(After the reading)
This is the Word of the Lord.
Thanks be to God.

PSALM/SCRIPTURAL SONG or HYMN

THE GOSPEL
Hear the Gospel of our Lord Jesus Christ according to N.
Glory to Christ our Saviour.

(After the reading)
This is the Gospel of the Lord.
Praise to you, O Christ.

THE SERMON

AFFIRMATION OF FAITH
Let us affirm our faith in God:

Do you believe and trust in God the Father, source of all being and life, the one for whom we exist?
We believe and trust in him.

Do you believe and trust in God the Son, who took our human nature, died for us and rose again?
We believe and trust in him.

Do you believe and trust in God the Holy Spirit, who gives life to the people of God and makes Christ known in the world?
We believe and trust in him.

This is the faith of the Church.
This is our faith.
We believe and trust in one God, Father, Son and Holy Spirit. **Amen.**

(A HYMN may be sung)

The Prayers

ROGATION THANKSGIVING
Creator God,
we give thanks for the wonder of Creation:
for the immense and the minute,
for gentle beauty and fierce grandeur,
for all the variety of place and season,
for fruitfulness in Nature and plentiful harvests.
We praise you.

For our heritage from generations past:
for landscape and garden,
for craft and skill,
for breed in livestock and variety in crops,
for wildlife untamed, for fertility renewed.
We praise you.

For those who act as stewards of God's creation,
for gardeners and foresters,
for crop and livestock farmers,
We praise you.

INTERCESSIONS
(Special thanksgivings and prayers …)

Father, we pray for farmers and fishermen, vets and merchants,
their families and rural communities;
for seasonable weather and good markets;
for those who are struggling to survive;
for rural churches and support groups,
Lord, in your mercy, **hear our prayer.**

For prosperity on farms, large and small;
for far-sightedness in government policies,
for care of the environment in farming practice, and for fairness in world trade,
Lord, in your mercy, **hear our prayer.**

For God's blessing on land and livestock,
and the ripening crops; for ourselves that we may receive our food with grateful hearts.
Lord, hear all our prayers for the sake of Jesus Christ our Lord. **Amen.**

THE LORD'S PRAYER
(A HYMN may be sung)

CONCLUDING PRAYER
May the road rise to meet you;
may the wind be always at your back,
may the rain fall softly upon your fields;
may God hold you in the hollow of his hand.
Amen. *(Gaelic blessing)*

(THE BLESSING or THE GRACE is said)

THE SEVENTH SUNDAY OF EASTER
SUNDAY AFTER ASCENSION DAY

'Jesus Christ ... exalted with great triumph to ... heaven'

Ascension Day (Latin *ascendare* – to go up) last Thursday marked the end of the 'Great Forty Days' since Easter, during which the risen Christ appeared to his disciples many times, culminating in his ascension to heaven. Now we look forward to celebrating his gift of the Holy Spirit at Pentecost (next Sunday). As Head of the Church and our great High Priest, Christ prays for us always. One day all will call him 'Lord'.

The Gathering

THE GREETING

Alleluia! Christ is risen.
He is risen indeed. Alleluia.

(A HYMN may be sung)

God also highly exalted him
**and gave him the name
that is above every name,**

so that at the name of Jesus
**every knee should bend in heaven
and on earth and under the earth,**

and every tongue should confess
**that Jesus Christ is Lord,
to the glory of God the Father.**
(Phil. 2:9-11)

PRAYER

God our Father, we give thanks
that you raised your Son from death to life,
and exalted him to your right hand in glory.
Send the Holy Spirit that we may
worship you, our Father,
and serve him, our Lord Jesus Christ.
Amen.

(SONGS may be sung)

* * * * *

PENITENCE

As we bow our heads in shame for our sins,
we remember that the ascended Christ, our
great High Priest in heaven, prays for us ...

Let us therefore approach the throne of
grace with boldness, so that we may receive
mercy, and find grace to help in time of
need. *(Heb. 4:16)*

When we have surrendered to the
temptations of the world, the flesh and the
devil ...
Lord, have mercy. **Lord, have mercy.**

When we have treated others with prejudice,
hatred or unconcern ...
Christ, have mercy. **Christ, have mercy.**

When we have served our own selfish
interests, rather than serve our ascended
King ...
Lord, have mercy. **Lord, have mercy.**

Almighty God,
who forgives all who truly repent,
have mercy upon *us*,
pardon and deliver *us* from all *our* sins,
confirm and strengthen *us* in all goodness,
and keep *us* in life eternal;
through Jesus Christ our Lord. **Amen.**

(The GLORIA, the VENITE, a SONG or RESPONSES may be used)

THE COLLECT OF THE DAY

Let us pray ... *(silent prayer)*

O God the King of glory,
you have exalted your only Son Jesus Christ
with great triumph to your Kingdom in
heaven: we beseech you, leave us not
comfortless,
but send your Holy Spirit to strengthen us
and exalt us to the place where our Saviour
Christ is gone before,
who is alive and reigns with you,
in the unity of the Holy Spirit,
one God, now and for ever. **Amen.**

The Liturgy of the Word

THE SCRIPTURE READING(S)

(After the reading)
This is the Word of the Lord.
Thanks be to God.

PSALM/SCRIPTURAL SONG or HYMN

THE GOSPEL

Hear the Gospel of our Lord Jesus Christ according to N.
Glory to Christ our Saviour.

(After the reading)
This is the Gospel of the Lord.
Praise to you, O Christ.

THE SERMON

AFFIRMATION OF FAITH

Let us affirm our faith in Jesus Christ the Son of God:

Though he was divine,
he did not cling to equality with God,
but made himself nothing.
Taking the form of a slave,
he was born in human likeness.
He humbled himself,
and was obedient to death –
even the death of the cross.
Therefore God has raised him on high,
and given him the name above every name: that at the name of Jesus
every knee should bow,
and every voice proclaim
that Jesus Christ is Lord,
to the glory of God the Father. Amen.
(Phil. 2:6-11)

This is the faith of the Church.
This is our faith.
We believe and trust in one God,
Father, Son and Holy Spirit. Amen.

(A HYMN may be sung)

The Prayers

INTERCESSIONS

(Special thanksgivings and prayers ...)

Father in heaven, we give thanks that your Son was raised from the humiliation of the cross to the glory of heaven. We offer our prayers through him who, as our great High Priest, ever intercedes for us.

We pray for all who serve his Church as bishops *(N.)*, priests, deacons and lay ministers ... Give them grace to nourish your people through spiritual worship, sound teaching and pastoral care.
Jesus, our High Priest, **hear our prayer.**

We pray for our Christian brothers and sisters in other places who are persecuted, hated or deprived ... Sustain their faith, and strengthen our fellowship with them through prayer and practical support.
Jesus, our High Priest, **hear our prayer.**

We pray for each other as we seek to be witnesses of Christ in our everyday lives and work ... Lead us by the Holy Spirit in the ways of Christ, that we may learn to speak and do as he would.
Jesus, our High Priest, **hear our prayer.**

We pray for our Queen and government, and for the leaders of the nations, as they try to resolve the difficult issues confronting them ... Make them know they are accountable to God and guide them into policies that promote justice, reconciliation and opportunity for all.
Jesus, our High Priest, **hear our prayer.**

We pray for those who face distressing illness, increasing frailty or painful treatment ... Bring healing through the care they receive from doctors and nurses, relatives and friends.
Jesus, our High Priest, **hear our prayer.**

We remember those who have died ...
Father raise us, with all who have died in faith, to eternal life in Christ. **Amen.**

THE LORD'S PRAYER

(A HYMN may be sung)

CONCLUDING PRAYER

Christ our ascended King, bestow on us your gifts, and bring us to glory. Amen.

(THE BLESSING or THE GRACE is said)

THE DAY OF PENTECOST
WHIT SUNDAY

Today we celebrate the gift of the Holy Spirit, 'the giver of life': Pentecost (Greek *Pentecoste* – fiftieth) was a Jewish harvest festival occurring 50 days after the Passover. It marked the occasion when, with signs of wind and flame, the Spirit came upon the first disciples. Now they were empowered to bear witness to Christ. 'Whit Sunday' refers to the white robes usually worn by those baptized on this day.

The Gathering

THE GREETING
The Lord is here.
His Spirit is with us.

(A HYMN may be sung)

Where can I go from your Spirit?
Or where can I flee from your presence?

If I ascend to heaven, you are there;
if I make my bed in Sheol, you are there.

If I take the wings of the morning and settle at the farthest limits of the sea,
*even there your hand shall lead me;
and your right hand shall hold me fast.*
(Ps. 139:7-10)

PRAYER
*Almighty God,
to whom all hearts are open,
all desires known,
and from whom no secrets are hidden:
cleanse the thoughts of our hearts
by the inspiration of your Holy Spirit,
that we may perfectly love you,
and worthily magnify your holy name;
through Christ our Lord.* **Amen.**

(SONGS may be sung)

* * * * *

PENITENCE
St Paul teaches us not to 'grieve the Holy Spirit of God'. *(Eph. 4:30)*
Let us therefore confess those sins that hinder his work among us ...

The Spirit brings us to life in Christ:
Lord, forgive us when we have closed our hearts to his renewing power.
Lord, have mercy. **Lord, have mercy.**

The Spirit leads us into the truth of Christ:
Lord, forgive us when we have closed our minds to learning anything new.
Christ, have mercy. **Christ, have mercy.**

The Spirit makes Christ known in the world:
Lord, forgive us when we have failed to bear witness to the gospel of Christ.
Lord, have mercy. **Lord, have mercy.**

Almighty God,
who forgives all who truly repent,
have mercy upon *us,*
pardon and deliver *us* from all *our* sins,
confirm and strengthen *us* in all goodness,
and keep *us* in life eternal;
through Jesus Christ our Lord. **Amen.**

(The GLORIA, the VENITE, a SONG or RESPONSES may be used)

THE COLLECT OF THE DAY
Let us pray ... *(silent prayer)*

God, who as at this time taught the hearts of your faithful people by sending to them the light of your Holy Spirit: grant us by the same Spirit to have a right judgement in all things and evermore to rejoice in his holy comfort; through the merits of Christ Jesus our Saviour, who is alive and reigns with you, in the unity of the Holy Spirit, one God, now and for ever. **Amen.**

The Liturgy of the Word

THE SCRIPTURE READING(S)

(After the reading)
This is the Word of the Lord.
Thanks be to God.

PSALM/SCRIPTURAL SONG or HYMN

THE GOSPEL

Hear the Gospel of our Lord Jesus Christ according to N.
Glory to you, O Lord.

(After the reading)
This is the Gospel of the Lord.
Praise to you, O Christ.

THE SERMON

AFFIRMATION OF FAITH

We believe in one God, the Father, the Almighty, maker of heaven and earth, of all that is, seen and unseen.

We believe in one Lord, Jesus Christ, the only Son of God, eternally begotten of the Father, God from God, Light from Light, true God from true God, begotten, not made, of one Being with the Father; through him all things were made.

**For us and for our salvation he came down from heaven, was incarnate from the Holy Spirit and the Virgin Mary, and was made man.
For our sake he was crucified under Pontius Pilate; he suffered death and was buried.
On the third day he rose again in accordance with the Scriptures; he ascended into heaven and is seated at the right hand of the Father.
He will come again in glory to judge the living and the dead, and his Kingdom will have no end.**

We believe in the Holy Spirit, the Lord, the giver of life, who proceeds from the Father and the Son, who with the Father and the Son is worshipped and glorified, who has spoken through the prophets.

**We believe in one holy catholic and apostolic Church. We acknowledge one baptism for the forgiveness of sins.
We look for the resurrection of the dead, and the life of the world to come. Amen.**

(The Nicene Creed)

(A HYMN may be sung)

The Prayers

INTERCESSIONS

(Special thanksgivings and prayers ...)

Friends and followers of Jesus, we rejoice because we share in his new life, and are led by the Spirit. We pray:

For bishop N. and for all clergy and lay ministers, that they will serve the Church with humility, holiness and inspiration ...
Holy Spirit of God, *renew us, we pray.*

For our Queen and government and the leaders of all nations, that they will promote peace and justice, freedom and human well-being
Holy Spirit of God, *renew us, we pray.*

For those places in the world where food is scarce, jobs are few or life is dangerous, that conditions will improve for all who struggle to survive ...
Holy Spirit of God, *renew us, we pray.*

For our families and all who are close to us, that in testing times they will be protected from harm and make the right choices ...
Holy Spirit of God, *renew us, we pray.*

For those who are ill, in pain, or undergoing treatment, that they will be healed ...
Holy Spirit of God, *renew us, we pray.*

For those parted from someone they love ...
May they be comforted in love, and lifted by hope, through Jesus Christ our Lord. **Amen.**

THE LORD'S PRAYER

(A HYMN may be sung)

CONCLUDING PRAYER

Let us live by the Spirit ... and not gratify the desires of the flesh ... May love, joy and peace blossom in our lives. **Amen.**

(Gal. 5:16, 22)

(THE BLESSING or THE GRACE is said)

TRINITY SUNDAY
'The glory of the eternal Trinity'

On Trinity Sunday (Latin/Greek *tri* – three) the Church glorifies God as Father, Son and Holy Spirit – three Persons in one God, three diverse expressions of God, working together in perfect unity. The **Father** sustains the world with *unconditional love*. The **Son** offers lost people *undeserved forgiveness*. The **Holy Spirit** gives Christ's followers *unlimited resources* to bear witness to God's Kingdom on earth.

The Gathering

THE GREETING
In the name of the Father and of the Son and of the Holy Spirit. **Amen.**

The Lord be with you.
And also with you.

(A HYMN may be sung)

IN PRAISE OF THE TRINITY
I bring these flowers
to remind me of the Father's love,
who made a world of such beauty and grace.
(Flowers in a vase are placed centrally)

I take up this cross
to remind me of the Son's forgiveness,
who endured the world's pain to set us free.
(A cross is placed centrally)

I light this candle
to remind me of the Spirit's power
who renews the Church for worship and witness.
(A candle is lit and placed centrally)

We gaze at these signs
of the Trinity of love:
God around us. God with us.
God among us:
the Beginning, the End,
the Everlasting One.

(SONGS may be sung)
* * * * *

PENITENCE
St Paul wrote 'All have sinned and fall short of the glory of God' ... *(Rom. 3:23)*

As we celebrate the holiness and goodness of God, we remember the shadows in our own lives:

Father God, we confess that we often take the gifts of your creation for granted, and use them chiefly to further our own interests ...
Lord, have mercy. **Lord, have mercy.**

Saviour Christ, we confess that we easily fall into temptation and forget to seek your forgiveness ...
Christ, have mercy. **Christ, have mercy.**

Holy Spirit, we confess that we often close our minds to your influence, and fail to bear good fruit in our lives ...
Lord, have mercy. **Lord, have mercy.**

May the Father forgive *us*
by the death of his Son
and strengthen *us*
to live in the power of the Spirit
all *our* days.   **Amen.**

(The GLORIA, the VENITE, a SONG or RESPONSES may be used)

THE COLLECT OF THE DAY
Let us pray ...   *(silent prayer)*

Almighty and everlasting God,
you have given us your servants grace, by the confession of a true faith, to acknowledge the glory of the eternal Trinity and in the power of the divine majesty to worship the Unity: keep us steadfast in this faith, that we may evermore be defended from all adversities;
through Jesus Christ your Son our Lord, who is alive and reigns with you,
in the unity of the Holy Spirit,
one God, now and for ever.   **Amen.**

The Liturgy of the Word

THE SCRIPTURE READING(S)

(After the reading)
This is the Word of the Lord.
Thanks be to God.

PSALM/HYMN or SCRIPTURAL SONG

THE GOSPEL

Hear the Gospel of our Lord Jesus Christ according to N.
Glory to you, O Lord.

(After the reading)
This is the Gospel of the Lord.
Praise to you, O Christ.

THE SERMON

AFFIRMATION OF FAITH

Let us affirm our faith in God:

**I believe in God, the Father almighty, creator of heaven and earth.
I believe in Jesus Christ, his only Son, our Lord, who was conceived by the Holy Spirit, born of the Virgin Mary, suffered under Pontius Pilate, was crucified, died, and was buried; he descended to the dead. On the third day he rose again; he ascended into heaven, he is seated at the right hand of the Father, and he will come to judge the living and the dead.
I believe in the Holy Spirit, the holy catholic Church, the communion of saints, the forgiveness of sins, the resurrection of the body, and the life everlasting.   Amen.**
(The Apostles' Creed)

(A HYMN may be sung)

The Prayers

INTERCESSIONS

(Special thanksgivings and prayers …)

God of the universe, Trinity of love, three Persons in one God, we praise you for your glory and grace. As your people, called to serve your Kingdom, we bring our prayers for the world.

Father of all, we pray for the whole human family, for our Queen, government and fellow-citizens, for the leaders of all the Nations …
Grant that the peoples of the world may learn to understand and respect each other, and work together to overcome injustice, poverty and conflict ...
God the Holy Trinity,   **hear our prayer.**

Jesus, Saviour of the world, we pray for the people whom you have redeemed. We pray for your Church, its bishops, clergy and lay ministers, for the young and old in faith, for our worship, learning and fellowship together.
Help us to be committed as your disciples, and bold as your witnesses in daily life.
God, the Holy Trinity,   **hear our prayer.**

Spirit of the living God, we remember all who are suffering in body, mind or spirit …
We pray for those who minister to them through care and medical skill. Bless all your people with gifts of faith, hope and love.
God, the Holy Trinity,   **hear our prayer.**

We give thanks for those who have died …
Father, Son and Holy Spirit grant us, with them, a share in your eternal Kingdom.
Amen.

THE LORD'S PRAYER

(A HYMN may be sung)

CONCLUDING PRAYER
Glory to the Father, and to the Son, and to the Holy Spirit; as it was in the beginning, is now, and shall be for ever.   Amen.

(THE BLESSING or THE GRACE is said)

THE FIRST SUNDAY AFTER TRINITY
'Grant us the help of your grace'

Grace, meaning 'favour' or 'gift' (translating the Latin *gratia* and the Greek *charis)* refers to God's unconditional love for the world, shown in the gifts he gives to the human race – life, food, intelligence, friendship and, above all, forgiveness and the new life in Christ. None of these things are earned or deserved. They are simply gifts – to be received humbly and gratefully.

The Gathering

THE GREETING
Grace, mercy and peace from God the Father and Christ Jesus our Lord be with you.   **And also with you.**   *(1 Tim. 1:2)*

(A HYMN may be sung)

By grace you have been saved through faith, and this is not your own doing:
it is the gift of God.   *(Eph. 2:8)*

God's love has been poured into our hearts **through the Holy Spirit that has been given to us.**   *(Rom. 5:5)*

PRAYER
Gracious God,
as we gather here to worship you,
make us thankful for your special gifts,
aware of our many failings,
humble to receive forgiveness,
and open to the Holy Spirit
who fills us with your life and love,
through Jesus Christ our Lord.   **Amen.**

(SONGS may be sung)
* * * * *

PENITENCE
The grace of God has appeared bringing salvation to all.   *(Titus 2:11)*

As we celebrate the grace and goodness of God, we remember our sins and weaknesses:

Father God, we confess that we often take the gifts of your creation for granted, and use them chiefly to further our own interests …
Lord, have mercy.   **Lord, have mercy.**

Saviour Christ, we confess that we often give in to the selfish desires of our hearts, and the uncaring ways of the world …
Christ, have mercy.   **Christ, have mercy.**

Holy Spirit, we confess that we often close our minds to your influence, and fail to bear good fruits in our lives …
Lord, have mercy.   **Lord, have mercy.**

May the Father forgive *us*
by the death of his Son
and strengthen *us*
to live in the power of the Spirit
all *our* days.   **Amen.**

(The GLORIA, the VENITE, a SONG or RESPONSES may be used)

THE COLLECT OF THE DAY
Let us pray …   *(silent prayer)*

O God, the strength of all those
who put their trust in you,
mercifully accept our prayers and,
because through the weakness
of our mortal nature
we can do no good thing without you,
grant us the help of your grace,
that in the keeping of your commandments
we may please you both in will and deed;
through Jesus Christ your Son our Lord,
who is alive and reigns with you,
in the unity of the Holy Spirit,
one God, now and for ever.   **Amen.**

The Liturgy of the Word

THE SCRIPTURE READING(S)
(After the reading)
This is the Word of the Lord.
Thanks be to God.

PSALM/HYMN or SCRIPTURAL SONG

THE GOSPEL
Hear the Gospel of our Lord Jesus Christ according to N.
Glory to you, O Lord.
(After the reading)
This is the Gospel of the Lord.
Praise to you, O Christ.

THE SERMON

AFFIRMATION OF FAITH
Let us declare our faith in God:

We believe in God the Father,
from whom every family
in heaven and on earth is named.

We believe in God the Son,
who lives in our hearts through faith,
and fills us with his love.

We believe in God the Holy Spirit,
who strengthens us
with power from on high.

We believe in one God;
Father, Son and Holy Spirit. Amen.
(from Eph. 3)

(A HYMN may be sung)

The Prayers

INTERCESSIONS
(Special thanksgivings and prayers …)

We pray to you our Father in heaven:

We give thanks for your grace that bestows on us many gifts of life and love, forgiveness and fortitude.
Renew us with the Holy Spirit.

We give thanks for all that we receive from the life and people of this church.
Inspire the bishops, clergy and lay ministers who serve your people.

We give thanks for Christ's call to follow him, and to bear witness to God's Kingdom.
Give us boldness to stand up for our beliefs, and perseverance in the face of hostility.

We give thanks for our country, our Queen and those who have authority in this and other nations.
Strengthen all leaders to serve the people with integrity, wisdom and faithfulness.

We give thanks for people of goodwill and high principles.
Bless all who promote justice and reconciliation throughout the world.

We give thanks for this astonishingly beautiful and bountiful world.
Give us the determination to protect it from abuse.

We give thanks for the support and care of our families and friends.
Enlarge our love to include those who are lonely or troubled.

We give thanks for what health we have.
Bring healing, patience and hope to those who suffer pain and infirmity.

We give thanks for those who have died, and pray for those left behind.
May we, with them, have a place in your eternal Kingdom.

Merciful Father, ***accept all these prayers in the name of your Son, Jesus Christ.***
Amen.

THE LORD'S PRAYER

(A HYMN may be sung)

CONCLUDING PRAYER
***Lord, we pray that your grace
may always precede and follow us,
and make us continually to be given
to all good works;
through Jesus Christ our Lord. Amen.***
(Collect from Common Worship)

(THE BLESSING or THE GRACE is said)

THE SECOND SUNDAY AFTER TRINITY
'Love – that most excellent gift'

Today's Collect speaks of love as 'that most excellent gift' from God. It was revealed supremely in the life, death and resurrection of Jesus Christ. It is experienced today through the Holy Spirit who guides and gifts Christ's followers. It is shown in those who love and serve their neighbour. It will be fully known when, at the end of our journey, we enter the eternal and perfect love of the Trinity – Father, Son and Holy Spirit.

The Gathering

THE GREETING
Grace, mercy and peace from God our Father and the Lord Jesus Christ be with you. **And also with you.** *(1 Tim. 1:2)*

(A HYMN may be sung)

God is love, and those who abide in love abide in God,
And God abides in them.

We love
because he first loved us. *(1 John 4:16, 19)*

PRAYER
Lord, you are the living flame,
burning ceaselessly with love for mankind.
Enter into us and inflame us with your love
so that we might be like you. **Amen.**
(J. H. Newman)

(SONGS may be sung)
* * * * *

PRAYERS OF PENITENCE
Let us examine our lives in the light of St Paul's teaching about the nature of love:

'Love is patient ... love is kind ...
is not envious ... or boastful ...
or arrogant ... or rude ...
does not insist on its own way ...
is not irritable ... or resentful
and does not rejoice in wrongdoing ...'
(1 Cor. 13:4-6)

Acknowledging that our attitudes and behaviour often fall short of these standards, we confess our sins to God:

Most merciful God,
Father of our Lord Jesus Christ,
we confess that we have sinned
in thought, word and deed.
We have not loved you with our
whole heart.
We have not loved our neighbours
as ourselves.
In your mercy
forgive what we have been,
help us to amend what we are,
and direct what we shall be;
that we may do justly, love mercy,
and walk humbly with you, our God.
Amen.

May almighty God have mercy on *us*
forgive *us our* sins,
and bring *us* to everlasting life,
through Jesus Christ our Lord. **Amen.**

(The GLORIA, the VENITE, a SONG or RESPONSES may be used)

THE COLLECT OF THE DAY
Let us pray ... *(silent prayer)*

Lord, you have taught us that all our doings without love are worth nothing: send your Holy Spirit and pour into our hearts that most excellent gift of love, the true bond of peace and of all virtues, without which whoever lives is counted dead before you.
Grant this for your only Son
Jesus Christ's sake,
who is alive and reigns with you,
in the unity of the Holy Spirit,
one God, now and for ever. **Amen.**

The Liturgy of the Word

THE SCRIPTURE READING(S)
(After the reading)
This is the Word of the Lord.
Thanks be to God.

PSALM/HYMN or SCRIPTURAL SONG

THE GOSPEL
Hear the Gospel of our Lord Jesus Christ according to N.
Glory to you, O Lord.

(After the reading)
This is the Gospel of the Lord.
Praise to you, O Christ.

THE SERMON

AFFIRMATION OF FAITH
Let us declare our faith in God:

**We believe in God the Father,
from whom every family
in heaven and on earth is named.**

**We believe in God the Son,
who lives in our hearts through faith,
and fills us with his love.**

**We believe in God the Holy Spirit,
who strengthens us
with power from on high.**

**We believe in one God;
Father, Son and Holy Spirit. Amen.**
(from Eph. 3)

(A HYMN may be sung)

The Prayers

INTERCESSIONS
(Special thanksgivings and prayers ...)

God our Father, we pray for your blessing on all people:

Bless our Queen and those who take authority in this and other nations ...
May they govern with wisdom and integrity, and bring justice and peace to the world.
Father of all, **in your mercy hear us.**

Bless those who lead the Church ...
May they be firm in faith, clear in vision, yet humble in your service:
Father of all, **in your mercy hear us.**

Bless those who teach, in schools, colleges and universities ...
May their skills help the young to achieve their best:
Father of all, **in your mercy hear us.**

Bless those who suffer from ill-health or pain, loneliness or loss ...
Deliver them from their distress and grant them healing, patience and peace ...
Father of all, **in your mercy hear us.**

Bless those who care for the sick and frail ...
May they bring strength and encouragement to others, and know your grace for themselves.
Father of all, **in your mercy hear us.**

Bless those who go out to work each day ...
May they use their gifts for the common good, and bear witness to Christ in the service they render:
Father of all, **in your mercy hear us.**

We remember with thanksgiving those who have died ...
Father of all, **grant us with them, and all the saints, a share in your eternal Kingdom, through Christ our Lord. Amen.**

THE LORD'S PRAYER

(A HYMN may be sung)

CONCLUDING PRAYER
Go before us, Lord, in all we do with your most gracious favour, and guide us with your continual help, that in all our works begun, continued and ended in you, we may glorify your holy name, and finally by your mercy receive everlasting life;
through Jesus Christ our Lord. **Amen.**
(Collect from Common Worship)

(THE BLESSING or THE GRACE is said)

THE THIRD SUNDAY AFTER TRINITY
'The glorious liberty of the children of God'

> The mission of Jesus Christ was to set people free, once and for all, from the destructive powers of sin, darkness and death, so that they might come under the loving rule of God. Therefore, by following Jesus and belonging to his Church we too are freed to live in the service of God, and to discover ultimately – in the words of today's Collect – 'the glorious liberty of the children of God'.

The Gathering

THE GREETING
O magnify the Lord with me
and let us exalt his name together.
(Ps. 34:3)

(A HYMN may be sung)

The Servant of God speaks of his mission:
'The Spirit of the Lord is upon me;
he has sent me to bring good news to the oppressed,
**to build up the broken-hearted
to proclaim liberty to the captives,
and release to the prisoners;**
to proclaim the year of the Lord's favour …'
(Isa. 61:1)

PRAYER
Heavenly Father, we thank you
for the beauty of the world around us;
for the love of family and friends,
for work and play, for food and clothes,
for the happiness of good times,
and the lessons from hard times.
Most of all we thank you for your grace
shown in Jesus Christ your Son,
who sets us free from sin's power,
so that we might serve in your Kingdom,
for his sake. **Amen.**

(SONGS may be sung)

* * * * *

PENITENCE
St. Paul wrestled with his own selfish tendencies. Using his words, let us confess our weaknesses and sins:
(from Rom. 7:19-20)

I do not do the good I want.
Lord, have mercy. **Lord, have mercy.**

But the evil I do not want is what I do.
Christ, have mercy. **Christ, have mercy.**

It is no longer I that do it
but sin that dwells within me.
Lord, have mercy. **Lord, have mercy.**

Wretched man that I am!
Who will rescue me from this body of death?
**Thanks be to God
through Jesus Christ our Lord!** Amen.

May the Father forgive *us*
by the death of his Son
and strengthen *us*
to live in the power of the Spirit
all *our* days. **Amen.**

(The GLORIA, the VENITE, a SONG or RESPONSES may be used)

THE COLLECT OF THE DAY
Let us pray … *(silent prayer)*

Almighty God,
you have broken the tyranny of sin
and have sent the Spirit of your Son
into our hearts whereby we call you Father:
give us grace to dedicate our freedom to
your service, that we and all creation
may be brought to the glorious liberty
of the children of God;
through Jesus Christ your Son our Lord
who is alive and reigns with you,
in the unity of the Holy Spirit,
one God, now and for ever. **Amen.**

The Liturgy of the Word

THE SCRIPTURE READING(S)

(After the reading)
This is the Word of the Lord.
Thanks be to God.

PSALM/HYMN SCRIPTURAL SONG

THE GOSPEL
Hear the Gospel of our Lord Jesus Christ according to N.
Glory to you, O Lord.

(After the reading)
This is the Gospel of the Lord.
Praise to you, O Christ.

THE SERMON

AFFIRMATION OF FAITH
We proclaim our faith in God:

Do you believe and trust in God the Father, source of all being and life, the one for whom we exist?
We believe and trust in him.

Do you believe and trust in God the Son who took our human nature, died for us, and rose again?
We believe and trust in him.

Do you believe and trust in God the Holy Spirit, who gives life to the people of God and makes Christ known in the world?
We believe and trust in him.

This is the faith of the Church.
This is our faith.
We believe and trust in one God;
Father, Son and Holy Spirit.   Amen.

(A HYMN may be sung)

The Prayers

INTERCESSIONS
(Special thanksgivings and prayers …)

Our Father in heaven, we bring you our prayers for the Church and for all people. Send your Holy Spirit to equip them with the gifts that are needed to serve you:

For our bishop N. and all ministers of God's word and sacraments, that they may serve your Church in love, and build up your people in truth and faith …
Let us pray to the Lord.   ***Lord, hear us.***

For the peace and well-being of the world, for our Queen and the leaders of the nations and for the resolution of deep and bitter conflicts …
Let us pray to the Lord.   ***Lord, hear us.***

For the innocent victims of violence or injustice, and for all who strive to overcome evil with good …
Let us pray to the Lord.   ***Lord, hear us.***

For our families and those close to us, and for all who need our time, our attention and our care …
Let us pray to the Lord.   ***Lord, hear us.***

For the sick, the suffering, the sorrowful and the dying, and for all who bring healing and hope to them …
Let us pray to the Lord.   ***Lord, hear us.***

We remember with thanksgiving those who have died …
Father of all,   ***grant us with them,***
and all the saints, a share in your eternal Kingdom, through Jesus Christ our Lord. Amen.

THE LORD'S PRAYER

(A HYMN may be sung)

CONCLUDING PRAYER
Almighty God,
we thank you for the gift of your holy Word.
May it be a lantern to our feet,
a light to our paths,
and a strength to our lives.
Take us and use us
to love and to serve
in the power of the Holy Spirit
and in the name of your Son,
Jesus Christ our Lord.   Amen.
(Collect from Common Worship)

(THE BLESSING or THE GRACE is said)

THE FOURTH SUNDAY AFTER TRINITY
'God, our Ruler and Guide'

> Some choices in life are straightforward, others more difficult. In life's journey, those who put their trust in God find – in the words of today's Collect – that God is 'our ruler and guide', who helps us pass through 'things temporal' (this world) while holding on to the 'things eternal' (faith, hope and love – in Christ).

The Gathering

THE GREETING
O Lord, open my lips:
and my mouth will declare your praise.
(Ps. 51:15)

(A HYMN may be sung)

Rejoice in the Lord always:
again I will say 'Rejoice'. *(Phil. 4:4)*

Sing psalms, hymns and spiritual songs to God. Do everything in the name of the Lord Jesus,
giving thanks to God the Father through him. *(Col. 3:16-17)*

**Heavenly Father,
in our time together now,
help us to sing of your glory,
learn from your Word,
trust in your grace
and grow strong in your service
through Jesus Christ our Lord. Amen.**

(SONGS may be sung)
* * * * *

PENITENCE
We reflect upon our lives, capable of so much good, but so often marred by wrong choices and selfish attitudes … *(silence)*

**Almighty and most merciful Father,
we have wandered and strayed from your ways like lost sheep.
We have followed too much the devices and desires of our own hearts.
We have offended against your holy laws.
We have left undone those things that we ought to have done;
and we have done those things that we ought not to have done
and there is no health in us.
But you, O Lord,
have mercy upon us in our need.
Spare those who confess their faults.
Restore those who are penitent,
according to your promises declared to mankind in Christ Jesus our Lord.
And grant, O most merciful Father,
for his sake, that from this time
we may live a disciplined, righteous and godly life,
to the glory of your holy name. Amen.**

May almighty God have mercy on *us*,
forgive *us our* sins,
and bring *us* to everlasting life,
through Jesus Christ our Lord. **Amen.**

(The GLORIA, the VENITE, a SONG or RESPONSES may be used)

THE COLLECT OF THE DAY
Let us pray … *(silent prayer)*

O God,
the protector of all who trust in you, without whom nothing is strong, nothing is holy
increase and multiply upon us your mercy;
that with you as our ruler and guide
we may so pass through things temporal that we lose not our hold on things eternal;
grant this, heavenly Father, for our Lord Jesus Christ's sake, who is alive and reigns with you, in the unity of the Holy Spirit,
one God, now and for ever. **Amen.**

The Liturgy of the Word

THE SCRIPTURE READING(S)
(After the reading)
This is the Word of the Lord.
Thanks be to God.

PSALM/HYMN or SCRIPTURAL SONG

THE GOSPEL
Hear the Gospel of our Lord Jesus Christ according to N.
Glory to you, O Lord.

(After the reading)
This is the Gospel of the Lord.
Praise to you, O Christ.

THE SERMON

AFFIRMATION OF FAITH
We proclaim the Church's faith in God:

Do you believe and trust in God the Father, source of all being and life, the one for whom we exist?
We believe and trust in him.

Do you believe and trust in God the Son who took our human nature, died for us, and rose again?
We believe and trust in him.

Do you believe and trust in God the Holy Spirit, who gives life to the people of God and makes Christ known in the world?
We believe and trust in him.

This is the faith of the Church.
This is our faith.
We believe and trust in one God;
Father, Son and Holy Spirit. *Amen.*

(A HYMN may be sung)

The Prayers

INTERCESSIONS
(Special thanksgivings and prayers …)

Father God, who knows our needs before we ask, hear our prayers for all people:

Give grace to those who minister in your Church: Bishop N., the clergy and all lay ministers … Anoint them with the Spirit for their work in building up the body of Christ.
Lord, in your mercy, **hear our prayer.**

Sustain our Christian brothers and sisters in other places who are persecuted … Deliver those who are in prison for their beliefs.
Lord, in your mercy, **hear our prayer.**

Guide our Queen and government and the leaders of the nations in all their decisions … Bring reconciliation to situations where there is deep and bitter conflict, and new opportunities for all to make the most of their lives.
Lord, in your mercy, **hear our prayer.**

Enlighten all who are engaged in scientific research. May their work promote the life, health and well-being of the world.
Lord, in your mercy, **hear our prayer.**

Bless the work of our local schools … Give teachers the skill, enthusiasm and patience to inspire the young to learn.
Lord, in your mercy, **hear our prayer.**

Be with those whose work is very demanding or unrewarding … Give employers understanding of their needs.
Lord, in your mercy, **hear our prayer.**

Be close to those who are unwell, frail or disabled … Bless all who bring healing and care, and who sustain hope.
Lord, in your mercy, **hear our prayer.**

We remember with thanksgiving those who have died … Strengthen all who grieve, with comfort, faith and peace, for Jesus' sake.
Amen.

THE LORD'S PRAYER

(A HYMN may be sung)

CONCLUDING PRAYER
Almighty and everlasting Father,
we thank you that you have brought us
safely to the beginning of this day.
Keep us from falling into sin
or running into danger;
order us in all our doings;
and guide us to do always
what is right in your eyes;
through Jesus Christ our Lord. *Amen.*
(Collect from Common Worship)

(THE BLESSING or THE GRACE is said)

THE FIFTH SUNDAY AFTER TRINITY
'Serve God in holiness and truth'

Jesus once said 'I am among you as one who serves' (Luke 22:27). His whole life was given up for the salvation of others, in the service of God's Kingdom. He calls us to share in the same mission: to reach out to people who are lost in their sin, pain or alienation with compassion, forgiveness and encouragement. Each of us has, as today's Collect puts it, a 'vocation and ministry' to serve others.

The Gathering

THE GREETING
Grace, mercy and peace from God the Father and Christ Jesus our Lord be with you.
And also with you. *(1 Tim. 1:2)*

(A HYMN may be sung)

Praise our God, all you his servants:
**and all who fear him,
both small and great.** *(Rev. 19:5)*

There are varieties of gifts:
but the same Spirit.
**There are varieties of service:
but the same Lord.**

There are varieties of activities:
**but it is the same God
who activates all of them.**
(1 Cor. 12:4-6)

PRAYER
God, our Father,
we are here to worship you
and to discover more of your love for us
through Jesus Christ.
Send the Holy Spirit to give us the strength
to serve others,
as he has served us,
for the sake of your Kingdom. **Amen.**

(SONGS may be sung)

* * * * *

PENITENCE
Jesus' Summary of the Law
(Mark 12:29-31)
The first commandment is:
'You shall love the Lord your God with all your heart, and with all your soul, and with all your mind, and with all your strength.'

The second is this:
'You shall love your neighbour as yourself.'

Let us confess our failures truly to serve God and our neighbour:

**Most merciful God,
Father of our Lord Jesus Christ,
we confess that we have sinned
in thought, word and deed.
We have not loved you with our
 whole heart.
We have not loved our neighbours
 as ourselves.
In your mercy
forgive what we have been,
help us to amend what we are,
and direct what we shall be;
that we may do justly, love mercy,
and walk humbly with you, our God.
Amen.**

May almighty God have mercy on *us*,
forgive *us* our sins,
and bring *us* to everlasting life,
through Jesus Christ our Lord. **Amen.**

(The GLORIA, the VENITE, a SONG or RESPONSES may be used)

THE COLLECT OF THE DAY
Let us pray ... *(silent prayer)*

Almighty and everlasting God,
by whose Spirit the whole body of the Church
is governed and sanctified:
hear our prayer
which we offer for all your faithful people,
that in their vocation and ministry
they may serve you in holiness and truth
to the glory of your name;
through our Lord and Saviour Jesus Christ,
who is alive and reigns with you,
in the unity of the Holy Spirit,
one God, now and for ever. **Amen.**

The Liturgy of the Word

THE SCRIPTURE READING(S)

(After the reading)
This is the Word of the Lord.
Thanks be to God.

PSALM/HYMN or SCRIPTURAL SONG

THE GOSPEL

Hear the Gospel of our Lord Jesus Christ according to N.
Glory to you, O Lord.

(After the reading)
This is the Gospel of the Lord.
Praise to you, O Christ.

THE SERMON

AFFIRMATION OF FAITH

Let us affirm our faith in Jesus Christ the Son of God:

Though he was divine,
he did not cling to equality with God,
but made himself nothing.
Taking the form of a slave,
he was born in human likeness.
He humbled himself, and was obedient
to death – even the death of the cross.
Therefore God has raised him on high,
and given him the name above every
name: that at the name of Jesus
every knee should bow,
and every voice proclaim
that Jesus Christ is Lord,
to the glory of God the Father.
(Phil. 2:6-11)

This is the faith of the Church.
This is our faith.
We believe and trust in one God,
Father, Son and Holy Spirit. Amen.

(A HYMN may be sung)

The Prayers

INTERCESSIONS

(Special thanksgivings and prayers …)

Father God,
by your grace we are your children:
through your Son we are redeemed from sin;
in the Spirit we are sent out as Christ's witnesses, and servants of your Kingdom.

We pray for the Church in its life and mission …
We pray for bishop N. and all ministers of the gospel …
We pray for new Christians, and those searching for you …
We pray for the suffering Church …
Make our lives bear witness to the gospel of Christ.
Lord, hear our prayer
and let our cry come to you.

We pray for the leaders of nations in the great responsibilities they bear …
We pray for our Queen and country …
We pray for the local community …
Make our lives to be of service to your Kingdom that is coming.
Lord, hear our prayer
and let our cry come to you.

We pray for people in need …
We pray for those who care for them …
Make us eager to help whoever needs us.
Lord, hear our prayer
and let our cry come to you.

We give thanks for all that is good in life.
Help us to appreciate each other's talents, and glorify God in the way we use them.

We remember with thanksgiving those who have died …
Grant us with them, and all the saints,
a share in your eternal Kingdom, through Jesus Christ our Lord. Amen.

THE LORD'S PRAYER

(A HYMN may be sung)

CONCLUDING PRAYER

Teach us good Lord,
to serve thee as thou deservest;
to give and not to count the cost,
to fight and not to heed the wounds,
to toil and not to seek for rest,
to labour and not to seek reward,
save that of knowing
that we do thy will. Amen.
(Ignatius Loyola)

(The BLESSING or the GRACE is said)

THE SIXTH SUNDAY AFTER TRINITY
'Loving God above all things'

Today's Collect prays that God, as if drawing from a huge reservoir of grace, will 'pour into our hearts' such love towards him that we will love him 'above all things'. What that means, as Jesus explained, is to love God 'with all your heart *(commitment)*, with all your soul *(longing)*, with all your mind *(thinking)*, and with all your strength *(serving)*', and to love your neighbour as yourself.

The Gathering

THE GREETING
Grace, mercy and peace to you from God the Father and Christ Jesus our Lord.
And also with you. *(1 Tim. 1:2)*

(A HYMN may be sung)

I will give thanks to the Lord with my whole heart:
I will tell of all your wonderful deeds.
(Ps. 9:1)
God's love has been poured into our hearts through the Holy Spirit that has been given to us. *(Rom. 5:5)*
Beloved, since God loved us so much, we also ought to love one another.
(1 John 4:11)

PRAYER
***Almighty God, to whom
all hearts are open, all desires known,
and from whom no secrets are hidden:
cleanse the thoughts of our hearts
by the inspiration of your Holy Spirit,
that we may perfectly love you,
and worthily magnify your holy name;
through Christ our Lord. Amen.***

(SONGS may be sung)

* * * * *

PENITENCE
Our Lord Jesus Christ said: The first commandment is this: 'Hear, O Israel, the Lord our God is the only Lord. You shall love the Lord your God with all your heart, with all your soul, with all your mind, and with all your strength.' The second is this: 'Love your neighbour as yourself.' There is no other commandment greater than these. On these two commandments hang all the law and the prophets. *(Matt. 22:37-39)*
Amen. Lord, have mercy.

We acknowledge that our love for God is sometimes half-hearted, and our love for our neighbour is sometimes unwilling …

Let us confess our sins, in penitence and faith, firmly resolved to keep God's commandments:
***Most merciful God,
Father of our Lord Jesus Christ, we confess that we have sinned in thought, word and deed. We have not loved you with our whole heart. We have not loved our neighbours as ourselves. In your mercy forgive what we have been, help us to amend what we are, and direct what we shall be; that we may do justly, love mercy, and walk humbly with you, our God. Amen.***

May almighty God have mercy on *us*, forgive *us our* sins,
and bring *us* to everlasting life, through Jesus Christ our Lord. ***Amen.***

(The GLORIA, the VENITE, a SONG or RESPONSES may be used)

THE COLLECT OF THE DAY
Let us pray … *(silent prayer)*

Merciful God, you have prepared for those who love you such good things as pass our understanding: pour into our hearts such love toward you that we, loving you in all things and above all things, may obtain your promises, which exceed all that we can desire; through Jesus Christ your Son our Lord, who is alive and reigns with you, in the unity of the Holy Spirit, one God, now and for ever. ***Amen.***

The Liturgy of the Word

THE SCRIPTURE READING(S)

(After the reading)
This is the Word of the Lord.
Thanks be to God.

PSALM/HYMN or SCRIPTURAL SONG

THE GOSPEL
Hear the Gospel of our Lord Jesus Christ according to N.
Glory to you, O Lord.

(After the reading)
This is the Gospel of the Lord.
Praise to you, O Christ.

THE SERMON

AFFIRMATION OF FAITH
Let us declare our faith in God:

We believe in God the Father,
from whom every family
in heaven and on earth is named.

We believe in God the Son,
who lives in our hearts through faith,
and fills us with his love.

We believe in God the Holy Spirit,
who strengthens us
with power from on high.

We believe in one God;
Father, Son and Holy Spirit. **Amen.**
(from Eph. 3)

(A HYMN may be sung)

The Prayers

INTERCESSIONS
(Special thanksgivings and prayers ...)

Our Father in heaven, we give thanks for the church and for all that we receive through its worship, teaching and fellowship. We pray:

for bishop N. and the life of this diocese ...
for each other here and all who minister among us ...
for our fellow Christians in other places ...
Renew us with the Holy Spirit that we may bear witness to Christ's love.
Lord, in your mercy, **hear our prayer.**

We give thanks for this nation and those in authority who serve the people with integrity and dedication. We pray:
for our Queen and government ...
for all who work in the media ...
for those suffering from disaster, war or oppression ...
Bring justice and harmony to all people, and new opportunities to make the most of their lives.
Lord, in your mercy, **hear our prayer.**

We give thanks for our community, for all who serve us, and those who cherish us ...
Strengthen the bonds of trust and respect within families, communities and workplaces ...
Lord, in your mercy, **hear our prayer.**

We give thanks for the health we have, and for the skills of those who attend to us when we are in need. Bring healing and encouragement to those suffering from ill-health, pain or frailty ...
Lord, in your mercy, **hear our prayer.**

We give thanks for those who have died and those whose memory is still treasured ...
Grant us, with them, and with all the saints
... the joy of eternal life
in Christ, our Lord. **Amen.**

THE LORD'S PRAYER

(A HYMN may be sung)

CONCLUDING PRAYER
O God,
you are the light of the minds that know you,
the life of the souls that love you,
and the strength of the wills that serve you:
help us to know you
that we may truly love you,
and so to love you
that we may truly serve you;
whom to serve is perfect freedom;
through Jesus Christ our Lord. **Amen.**
(St Augustine)

(THE BLESSING or THE GRACE is said)

THE SEVENTH SUNDAY AFTER TRINITY
'The Author and Giver of all good things'

God is addressed, in today's Collect, as 'the author and giver of all good things'. This reminds us that the world exists, not because of mere chance, but because God planned and created it in the beginning. We gather together here to celebrate the gifts of creation and redemption, asking God to 'graft in our hearts the love of your name'.

The Gathering

THE GREETING
The Lord of glory be with you:
The Lord bless you.

(A HYMN may be sung)

Creator God, we give you thanks for your gifts:
for summer warmth and cooling breezes
we give you thanks and praise.

For refreshing rain and ripening crops
we give you thanks and praise.

For towering trees and fragrant blossom
we give you thanks and praise.

For mighty oceans and endless sky
we give you thanks and praise.

For all living creatures that share our earthly home
we give you thanks and praise.

For family relationships and friends we trust
we give you thanks and praise.   Amen.

PRAYER
Almighty God,
to whom all hearts are open,
all desires known,
and from whom no secrets are hidden:
cleanse the thoughts of our hearts
by the inspiration of your Holy Spirit,
that we may perfectly love you,
and worthily magnify your holy name;
through Christ our Lord.   Amen.

(SONGS may be sung)
* * * * *

PENITENCE
As we think of the many gifts God bestows on us, we also remember the many times we have taken them for granted, or squandered them in use ...
Let us confess our sins, in penitence and faith:
Almighty God, our heavenly Father,
we have sinned against you
and against our neighbour
in thought and word and deed,
through negligence, through weakness,
through our own deliberate fault.
We are truly sorry
and repent of all our sins.
For the sake of your Son Jesus Christ,
who died for us,
forgive us all that is past and grant
that we may serve you in newness of
life to the glory of your name.   Amen.

May the Father forgive *us*
by the death of his Son
and strengthen *us*
to live in the power of the Spirit
all our days.   **Amen.**

(The GLORIA, the VENITE, a SONG or RESPONSES may be used)

THE COLLECT OF THE DAY
Let us pray ...   *(silent prayer)*

Lord of all power and might,
the author and giver of all good things:
graft in our hearts the love of your name,
increase in us true religion, nourish us with all goodness, and of your great mercy keep us in the same;
through Jesus Christ your Son our Lord,
who is alive and reigns with you,
in the unity of the Holy Spirit,
one God, now and for ever.   **Amen.**

The Liturgy of the Word

THE SCRIPTURE READING(S)

(After the reading)
This is the Word of the Lord.
Thanks be to God.

PSALM/HYMN or SCRIPTURAL SONG

THE GOSPEL
Hear the Gospel of our Lord Jesus Christ according to N.
Glory to you, O Lord.

(After the reading)
This is the Gospel of the Lord.
Praise to you, O Christ.

THE SERMON

AFFIRMATION OF FAITH
We affirm our faith in God:
Do you believe and trust in God the Father, source of all being and life, the one for whom we exist?
We believe and trust in him.

Do you believe and trust in God the Son who took our human nature, died for us, and rose again?
We believe and trust in him.

Do you believe and trust in God the Holy Spirit, who gives life to the people of God and makes Christ known in the world?
We believe and trust in him.

This is the faith of the Church.
This is our faith.
We believe in one God;
Father, Son and Holy Spirit.   Amen.

(A HYMN may be sung)

The Prayers

INTERCESSIONS
(Special thanksgivings and prayers ...)

God, our loving heavenly Father, who hears the prayers of your children, we pray for the Church and for all people:

For bishop N. and the life of this diocese ... for those who minister among us here, and for our shared activities of worship, learning and fellowship in Christ ...
Father,   **hear the prayer we offer.**

For our Queen, the Prime Minister, members of the Cabinet, and for the leaders of all nations, as they tackle the challenges that face the human family – conflict and terrorism, injustice and poverty, natural disasters and environmental damage ...
Father,   **hear the prayer we offer.**

For public employers and private firms, for the local business sector, and for all who use their talents and energies to serve the needs of clients ...
Father,   **hear the prayer we offer.**

For all places of education in our neighbourhood, for those who teach in them and the young as they respond to the learning opportunities they are given ...
Father,   **hear the prayer we offer.**

For those who have become dependent upon drugs, alcohol or other addictive influences, and for their families and health workers who patiently encourage them along the path of liberation ...
Father,   **hear the prayer we offer.**

For people who have health needs, painful symptoms, or disabilities ... Give them strength, patience and relief, and bless all who support them.
Father,   **hear the prayer we offer.**

We remember with thanksgiving those who have died and pray for their loved ones in their bereavement and loneliness ...
Grant us, with them and with N. and all the saints, a share in your eternal Kingdom, through Jesus Christ our Lord.   **Amen.**

THE LORD'S PRAYER

(A HYMN may be sung)

CONCLUDING PRAYER
God our Father,
be with those who travel by land or sea or air, and all who are on holiday at this time, and bring them safely to their journey's end, through Jesus Christ our Lord.   **Amen.**

(THE BLESSING or THE GRACE is said)

THE EIGHTH SUNDAY AFTER TRINITY
'God's most mighty protection'

> Today's Collect prays that 'through God's most mighty protection ... we may be preserved in body and soul'. This is a prayer asking, not just for personal safety, but that God's unfailing care will enable us to do 'the works of his commandments'. Someone else put it like this: 'Lord, keep me under your protection till my work is done, and in your service till my life shall end.'

The Gathering

THE GREETING
Grace, mercy and peace to you from God
the Father and Christ Jesus our Lord.
And also with you. *(1 Tim. 1:2)*

(A HYMN may be sung)

Protect me, O God, for in you I take refuge.
***I say to the Lord, 'You are my Lord; I have
no good apart from you.'***
You show me the path of life.
In your presence
there is fullness of joy;
***In your right hand
are pleasures for evermore.***
(Ps. 16:1, 11)

PRAYER
Loving Father,
who on a day like this, the first day of the
week, raised your Son Jesus Christ
from death to life,
raise us up from the darkness of our sins
to praise you with all your saints.
Send your Spirit upon us
that our lives may be renewed in love
for Jesus' sake. **Amen.**

(SONGS may be sung)

* * * * *

PENITENCE
Remembering that sin damages our
relationships, let us bring our lives into
the pure light of God that he may cleanse us:

If we walk in the light,
as God himself is in the light,
we have fellowship with one another,
***and the blood of Jesus, his Son
cleanses us from all sin.*** *(1 John 1:7)*

Gracious God,
we pretend to be good when we are not ...
How quick we are to find fault in others.
Lord, have mercy. **Lord, have mercy.**

Merciful Lord,
we often turn our backs on those who need
us. How slow we are to do good.
Christ, have mercy. **Christ, have mercy.**

Holy God,
we often place our needs and desires
above everything else.
How reluctant we are to seek your will.
Lord, have mercy. **Lord, have mercy.**

Almighty God,
who forgives all who truly repent,
have mercy upon *us,*
pardon and deliver *us* from all *our* sins,
confirm and strengthen *us* in all goodness,
and keep *us* in life eternal;
through Jesus Christ our Lord. **Amen.**

*(The GLORIA, the VENITE, a SONG or
RESPONSES may be used)*

THE COLLECT OF THE DAY
Let us pray ... *(silent prayer)*

Almighty Lord and everlasting God,
we beseech you to direct, sanctify and
govern both our hearts and bodies in the
ways of your laws and the works of your
commandments; that through your most
mighty protection, both here and ever,
we may be preserved in body and soul;
through our Lord and Saviour Jesus Christ,
who is alive and reigns with you, in the unity
of the Holy Spirit, one God, now and for
ever. **Amen.**

The Liturgy of the Word

THE SCRIPTURE READING(S)

(After the reading)
This is the Word of the Lord.
Thanks be to God.

PSALM/HYMN or SCRIPTURAL SONG

THE GOSPEL

Hear the Gospel of our Lord Jesus Christ according to N.
Glory to you, O Lord.

(After the reading)
This is the Gospel of the Lord.
Praise to you, O Christ.

THE SERMON

AFFIRMATION OF FAITH

Let us affirm our faith in God:

**I believe in God, the Father almighty, creator of heaven and earth.
I believe in Jesus Christ, his only Son, our Lord, who was conceived by the Holy Spirit, born of the Virgin Mary, suffered under Pontius Pilate, was crucified, died and was buried; he descended to the dead.
On the third day he rose again; he ascended into heaven, he is seated at the right hand of the Father, and he will come to judge the living and the dead.
I believe in the Holy Spirit, the holy catholic Church, the communion of saints, the forgiveness of sins, the resurrection of the body, and the life everlasting. Amen.**
(The Apostles' Creed)

(A HYMN may be sung)

The Prayers

INTERCESSIONS

(Special thanksgivings and prayers ...)

We bring to you, Father God, the needs of all people, for whose salvation you sent your Son Jesus Christ:

We pray for our Queen and government, and the leaders of the nations ... We think of people divided by national enmity, religious intolerance, or racial prejudice ...
Lord Jesus, where there is hatred,
let me sow love.

We pray for husbands and wives, parents and children, employers and employees ... We think of families, communities and work places where relationships have broken down ...
Lord Jesus, where there is injury,
let me sow pardon.

We pray for bishop N., for all who teach the Christian faith, and for the life of our Church ... We think of those whose faith is being sorely tested ...
Lord Jesus, where there is doubt
let me sow faith.

We remember with thanksgiving those who have died ... We think of those who are overshadowed by loss or loneliness ... We pray for all in need ... We pray for their families and friends, doctors, nurses and carers.
Lord Jesus, where there is despair,
let me give hope.

We think of ourselves, our self-centredness, our faltering attempts to serve you ...
Lord Jesus,
make us channels of your peace and witnesses of your Kingdom. Amen.

THE LORD'S PRAYER

(A HYMN may be sung)

CONCLUDING PRAYER

Lord, be thou a bright flame before me.
Be thou a guiding star above me.
Be thou a smooth path below me.
Be thou a kindly shepherd behind me.
Today – tonight – and forever. **Amen.**
(St Columba)

(THE BLESSING or THE GRACE is said)

THE NINTH SUNDAY AFTER TRINITY
'Bring forth the fruit of the Spirit'

> The Holy Spirit, according to today's Collect, is 'the life and light of the Church'. He pours upon God's people gifts of love, energy and knowledge of Christ. The resulting 'fruit' includes 'love, joy and peace'. Let us pray that we will 'open our hearts' afresh to the wind of the Spirit and become more fruitful in Christ's service.

The Gathering

THE GREETING
Grace, mercy and peace to you from God
the Father and Christ Jesus our Lord.
And also with you. *(1 Tim. 1:2)*

(A HYMN may be sung)

St Paul wrote:
Live by the Spirit, I say,
and do not gratify the desires of the flesh.

The fruit of the Spirit is love, joy, peace …
**If we live by the Spirit,
let us also be guided by the Spirit.**
(Gal. 5:16, 22-23, 25)

PRAYER
**Almighty God,
to whom all hearts are open,
all desires known,
and from whom no secrets are hidden:
cleanse the thoughts of our hearts
by the inspiration of your Holy Spirit,
that we may perfectly love you,
and worthily magnify your holy name;
through Christ our Lord. Amen.**

(SONGS may be sung)
* * * * *

PENITENCE
In the presence of our holy and merciful
Lord, we measure our Christian lives against
the nine-fold fruits listed by St Paul.
(Gal. 5:22-23)

'The fruit of the Spirit is love, joy and peace.'
Forgive us, Lord, when we have pursued our
own interests rather than the things that
make for peace.
Lord, have mercy. **Lord, have mercy.**

'The fruit of the Spirit is patience, kindness
and generosity.'
Forgive us, Lord, when we have been
intolerant of other people's failings, or
uncaring about their needs.
Christ, have mercy. **Christ, have mercy.**

'The fruit of the spirit is faithfulness,
gentleness and self-control.'
Forgive us, Lord, when we have let people
down, or failed to place our trust in you.
Lord, have mercy. **Lord, have mercy.**

May almighty God have mercy on *us*,
forgive *us our* sins,
and bring *us* to everlasting life,
through Jesus Christ our Lord. **Amen.**

*(The GLORIA, the VENITE, a SONG or
RESPONSES may be used)*

THE COLLECT OF THE DAY
Let us pray … *(silent prayer)*

Almighty God,
who sent your Holy Spirit
to be the life and light of your Church:
open our hearts to the riches of your grace,
that we may bring forth the fruit of the Spirit
in love and joy and peace;
through Jesus Christ your Son our Lord,
who is alive and reigns with you,
in the unity of the Holy Spirit,
one God, now and for ever. **Amen.**

The Liturgy of the Word

THE SCRIPTURE READING(S)

(After the reading)
This is the Word of the Lord.
Thanks be to God.

PSALM/HYMN or SCRIPTURAL SONG

THE GOSPEL
Hear the Gospel of our Lord Jesus Christ according to N.
Glory to you, O Lord.

(After the reading)
This is the Gospel of the Lord.
Praise to you, O Christ.

THE SERMON

AFFIRMATION OF FAITH
Let us affirm our faith in God:

Do you believe and trust in God the Father, source of all being and life, the one for whom we exist?
We believe and trust in him.

Do you believe and trust in God the Son who took our human nature, died for us, and rose again?
We believe and trust in him.

Do you believe and trust in God the Holy Spirit, who gives life to the people of God and makes Christ known in the world?
We believe and trust in him.

This is the faith of the Church.
**This is our faith.
We believe and trust in one God,
Father, Son and Holy Spirit.   Amen.**

(A HYMN may be sung)

The Prayers

INTERCESSIONS
(Special thanksgivings and prayers ...)

Our Father in heaven, we pray for all people, in the name of your Son Jesus Christ:

We pray for the Church, for bishop N., and for all who lead, teach and minister in Christ's name ... Grant that we may be nourished in our faith and understanding, and bear daily witness to Christ's love.
Lord of life,   ***in your mercy, hear us.***

We pray for the nations of the world and for those who take authority to serve the cause of justice and human well-being ... Strengthen our Queen and the leaders of the nations with gifts of wisdom, courage and integrity, that your will may be done on earth as it is in heaven.
Lord of life,   ***in your mercy, hear us.***

We pray for those who are afflicted by natural disasters, or caught up in brutal conflicts ...
Fill them with the resurrection hope that good will prevail, and bless all who stand with them in finding solutions to their difficulties.
Lord of life,   ***in your mercy, hear us.***

We pray for the people we are called to serve, in the home, the neighbourhood and at work ... Help us to work hard at building good relationships, and to strive for reconciliation when they break down.
Lord of life,   ***in your mercy, hear us.***

We pray for all who suffer from illness, loneliness or weakness ... Raise them from despair to hopefulness and health.
Lord of life,   ***in your mercy, hear us.***

We remember with thanksgiving those who have died ... Strengthen all who mourn, with the sure hope that, in Christ, their loved ones are raised to fullness of life.
Lord of life,   ***in your mercy, hear us.***

**Accept all these prayers for the sake of your Son our Saviour Jesus Christ.
                                     Amen.**

THE LORD'S PRAYER

(A HYMN may be sung)

CONCLUDING PRAYER
If we sow to the Spirit, we will reap eternal life from the Spirit.
**Lord, let us not grow weary in doing what is right, for we will reap at harvest time, if we do not give up,
for Jesus' sake. Amen.**   *(Gal. 5:8-9)*

(THE BLESSING or THE GRACE is said)

THE TENTH SUNDAY AFTER TRINITY
'Praying which pleases God'

Prayer is not just a matter of asking God for the help we want. It is also about seeking, and praying for, what God wants – which might be quite different. Today's Collect reflects both these aspects: '… Lord, be open to the prayers of your humble servants, and … make them to ask such things as shall please you.'

The Gathering

THE GREETING
Grace, mercy and peace to you from God the Father and Christ Jesus our Lord.
And also with you. *(1 Tim. 1:2)*

(A HYMN may be sung)

Jesus said: Ask, and it will be given you;
search, and you will find;
knock, and the door will be opened for you.
For everyone who asks receives,
and everyone who searches finds,
and for everyone who knocks,
the door will be opened.
If you know how to give good gifts to your children,
how much more will the heavenly Father give the Holy Spirit to those who ask him!
(Luke 11:9-10, 13)

PRAYER
Lord Jesus Christ,
give us the desire to seek first
God's will in all things.
Grant us the honesty to confess our sins,
and the humility to receive your forgiveness.
Help us to listen to your Word,
and show forth your love,
in lives of service and sacrifice. **Amen**

(SONGS may be sung)
* * * * *

PENITENCE
In God's holy presence let us examine the words of our mouths, the deeds of our bodies, and the desires of our minds, confessing our sins to him …

When we are quick to criticize others, but slow to praise them …
Lord, have mercy. **Lord, have mercy.**

When we bear grudges, and find it hard to forgive …
Christ, have mercy. **Christ, have mercy.**

When we think we alone are right, and impose our views on others …
Lord, have mercy. **Lord, have mercy.**

When we let evil go unchallenged, and are afraid to speak the truth …
Christ, have mercy. **Christ, have mercy.**

When we are preoccupied with ourselves, and give little attention to others …
Lord, have mercy. **Lord, have mercy.**

When we trust in material things, more than in God's unfailing love …
Christ, have mercy. **Christ, have mercy.**

May almighty God have mercy on *us*,
forgive *us our* sins,
and bring *us* to everlasting life,
through Jesus Christ our Lord. **Amen.**

(The GLORIA, the VENITE, a SONG or RESPONSES may be used)

THE COLLECT OF THE DAY
Let us pray … *(silent prayer)*

Let your merciful ears, O Lord,
be open to the prayers of your humble servants;
and that they may obtain their petitions make them to ask such things
as shall please you;
through Jesus Christ your Son our Lord,
who is alive and reigns with you,
in the unity of the Holy Spirit,
one God, now and for ever. **Amen.**

The Liturgy of the Word

THE SCRIPTURE READING(S)

(After the reading)
This is the Word of the Lord.
Thanks be to God.

PSALM/HYMN or SCRIPTURAL SONG

THE GOSPEL
Hear the Gospel of our Lord Jesus Christ according to N.
Glory to you, O Lord.

(After the reading)
This is the Gospel of the Lord.
Praise to you, O Christ.

THE SERMON

AFFIRMATION OF FAITH
Let us proclaim our faith in God:

Do you believe and trust in God the Father, source of all being and life, the one for whom we exist?
We believe and trust in him.

Do you believe and trust in God the Son who took our human nature, died for us, and rose again?
We believe and trust in him.

Do you believe and trust in God the Holy Spirit, who gives life to the people of God and makes Christ known in the world?
We believe and trust in him.

This is the faith of the Church.
This is our faith.
We believe and trust in one God,
Father, Son and Holy Spirit. Amen.

(A HYMN may be sung)

The Prayers

INTERCESSIONS
(Special thanksgivings and prayers ...)

Father in heaven, we pray that your will may be done on earth as in heaven:

We pray for the Church: for bishop N., for ministers and all your people; for the Holy Spirit's gifts as we seek to serve you; for wisdom and courage as we communicate the Gospel to people who have no room for God; for growth in commitment among us ...
Father, your Kingdom come,
your will be done.

We pray for our Queen and country, and for all the nations of the world: for leaders who are dedicated to serving the people; for wisdom as they deal with difficult issues; for reconciliation where there is hatred and conflict; for justice to the poor and the excluded ...
Father, your Kingdom come,
your will be done.

We pray for the people among whom we live and work: for our families who need our time and affection; for any friends who feel hurt or let down; for the neighbours who long for someone to call; for those at work who suffer from stress or poor management ...
Father, your Kingdom come,
your will be done.

We pray for all whose lives are blighted by illness, pain or frailty; for all who are enslaved to addictive habits; for all who find life bleak without the person they love; for all who bring care, encouragement and healing to those who suffer ...
Father, your Kingdom come,
your will be done.

We remember with thanksgiving those who have died ... and commend them and all people to your mercy and peace,
through Jesus Christ our Lord. **Amen.**

THE LORD'S PRAYER

(A HYMN may be sung)

CONCLUDING PRAYER
The Father's love enfold us,
the grace of Christ uphold us,
the Holy Spirit guide us;
one God to walk beside us. Amen.

(THE BLESSING or THE GRACE is said)

THE ELEVENTH SUNDAY AFTER TRINITY

'God's power is shown chiefly in his mercy'

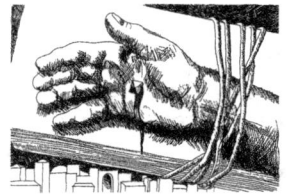

At the heart of the Christian gospel is the truth that the almighty, all-powerful God came among us, in the weakness of our human flesh, to show – as today's Collect puts it – his mercy and pity. Through his Son Jesus Christ, he forgives our sins and gives us grace to 'run the way of his commandments' and share in his 'heavenly treasure' – eternal life in Christ.

The Gathering

THE GREETING
Grace, mercy and peace to you from God the Father and Christ Jesus our Lord.
And also with you. *(1 Tim. 1:2)*

(A HYMN may be sung)

This is the day that the Lord has made.
Let us rejoice and be glad in it.

You are my God, and I will give thanks to you;
you are my God, I will extol you.

O give thanks to the Lord, for he is good,
for his steadfast love endures for ever.
(Ps. 118:24, 28-29)

PRAYER
*Almighty God,
to whom all hearts are open,
all desires known
and from whom no secrets are hidden:
cleanse the thoughts of our hearts
by the inspiration of your Holy Spirit,
that we may perfectly love you,
and worthily magnify your holy name;
through Christ our Lord.* **Amen.**

(SONGS may be sung)
* * * * *

PRAYER OF PENITENCE
Hear the words of comfort our Saviour Christ says to all who truly turn to him:
'Come to me, all who labour and are heavy laden, and I will give you rest.' (Matt. 11:28)
'God so loved the world that he gave his only-begotten Son, that whoever believes in him should not perish but have eternal life.'
(John 3:16)
Hear what St Paul says: 'This saying is true and worthy of full acceptance, that Christ Jesus came into the world to save sinners.'
(1 Tim. 1:15)
Let us confess our sins, in penitence and faith, firmly resolved to keep God's commandments and to live in love and peace with all.

*Almighty God, our heavenly Father,
we have sinned against you
and against our neighbour
in thought and word and deed,
through negligence, through weakness,
through our own deliberate fault.
We are truly sorry
and repent of all our sins.
For the sake of your Son Jesus Christ,
who died for us,
forgive us all that is past and grant
that we may serve you in newness of
life to the glory of your name.* **Amen.**

May almighty God have mercy on *us*,
forgive *us* our sins,
and bring *us* to everlasting life,
through Jesus Christ our Lord. **Amen.**

(The GLORIA, the VENITE, a SONG or RESPONSES may be used)

THE COLLECT OF THE DAY
Let us pray … *(silent prayer)*

O God, you declare your almighty power most chiefly in showing mercy and pity; mercifully grant to us such a measure of your grace, that we, running the way of your commandments, may receive your gracious promises, and be made partakers of your heavenly treasure; through Jesus Christ your Son our Lord, who is alive and reigns with you, in the unity of the Holy Spirit, one God, now and for ever. **Amen.**

The Liturgy of the Word

THE SCRIPTURE READING(S)

(After the reading)
This is the Word of the Lord.
Thanks be to God.

PSALM/HYMN or SCRIPTURAL SONG

THE GOSPEL

Hear the Gospel of our Lord Jesus Christ according to N.
Glory to you, O Lord.

(After the reading)
This is the Gospel of the Lord.
Praise to you, O Christ.

THE SERMON

AFFIRMATION OF FAITH

**I believe in God, the Father almighty, creator of heaven and earth.
I believe in Jesus Christ, his only Son, our Lord, who was conceived by the Holy Spirit, born of the Virgin Mary, suffered under Pontius Pilate, was crucified, died, and was buried; he descended to the dead. On the third day he rose again; he ascended into heaven, he is seated at the right hand of the Father, and he will come to judge the living and the dead.
I believe in the Holy Spirit, the holy catholic Church, the communion of saints, the forgiveness of sins, the resurrection of the body, and the life everlasting. Amen.**
(The Apostles' Creed)

(A HYMN may be sung)

The Prayers

INTERCESSIONS

(Special thanksgivings and prayers ...)

Father God, we pray for your holy catholic apostolic Church;
that we may all be one in Christ, our risen Saviour.

Grant that every member of the Church may grow in knowledge of you, and faithfully serve you;
that your Kingdom may come and your will be done.

We pray for bishop N., all clergy and lay workers;
that they may be faithful ministers of your truth and grace.

We pray for our Queen and all who hold authority in the nations of the world;
that there may be justice and peace on the earth.

Give us grace to do your will in all that we plan and do;
that our works may bring glory to your Name.

Fill us with compassion for those who suffer from any grief, trouble or injustice;
that they may be delivered from distress.

We remember with thanksgiving those who have died ...
We praise your for your saints who have entered into eternal rest;
may we also come to share in your eternal joy.

In a moment of silence, let us pray for those we most deeply care about ...
Merciful Father,
accept all these prayers for the sake of your Son, our Saviour Jesus Christ.
Amen.

THE LORD'S PRAYER

(A HYMN may be sung)

CONCLUDING PRAYER

Grant, Lord, that we may hold to you without parting, worship without wearying, serve you without failing; faithfully seek you, happily find you, and for ever possess you, the only God, blessed now and always. Amen. *(St Anselm)*

(THE BLESSING or THE GRACE is said)

THE TWELFTH SUNDAY AFTER TRINITY
'God is ready to give more than we desire or deserve'

The Collect today reminds us of the astonishingly generous gifts of God. They are 'more than either we desire or deserve', and include Christ's forgiveness of our sins and the Spirit's unlimited resources. But this 'grace' of God is also experienced in everyday events – such as the care given and received in close human relationships. We celebrate God's grace in our worship together now.

The Gathering

THE GREETING
The grace and mercy of our Lord Jesus Christ be with you.
And also with you.

(A HYMN may be sung)

God's love has been poured into our hearts **through the Holy Spirit that has been given to us.** *(Rom. 5:5)*

See what love the Father has given us, **that we should be called children of God; and that is what we are.**

Little children, let us love, not in word or speech,
but in truth and action.
(1 John 3:1, 18)

PRAYER
**Lord, you are the living flame,
burning ceaselessly
with love for mankind.
Enter into us
and inflame us with your love
so that we might be like you.   Amen.**
(J. H. Newman)

(SONGS may be sung)

* * * * *

PENITENCE
In a moment of quiet we think of the many gifts of God:
life, food, health, shelter, talents …
the love we receive from others …
and the grace we receive from Christ …
As we celebrate the goodness of God, we also remember the shadows in our lives:

Father God, we confess that we often take the gifts of your creation for granted, and use them chiefly to further our own interests …
Lord, have mercy.   **Lord, have mercy.**

Saviour Christ, we confess that we easily fall into temptation and forget to seek your forgiveness …
Christ, have mercy.   **Christ, have mercy.**

Holy Spirit, we confess that we often close our minds to your influence, and fail to bear good fruit in our lives …
Lord, have mercy.   **Lord, have mercy.**

May the Father forgive *us*
by the death of his Son
and strengthen *us*
to live in the power of the Spirit
all *our* days.   **Amen.**

(The GLORIA, the VENITE, a SONG or RESPONSES may be used)

THE COLLECT OF THE DAY
Let us pray …   *(silent prayer)*

Almighty and everlasting God,
you are always more ready to hear than we to pray and to give more than either we desire or deserve: pour down upon us the abundance of your mercy, forgiving us those things of which our conscience is afraid and giving us those good things which we are not worthy to ask but through the merits and mediation of Jesus Christ your Son our Lord, who is alive and reigns with you, in the unity of the Holy Spirit, one God, now and for ever.   **Amen.**

The Liturgy of the Word

THE SCRIPTURE READING(S)

(After the reading)
This is the Word of the Lord.
Thanks be to God.

PSALM/HYMN or SCRIPTURAL SONG

THE GOSPEL
Hear the Gospel of our Lord Jesus Christ according to N.
Glory to you, O Lord.

(After the reading)
This is the Gospel of the Lord.
Praise to you, O Christ.

THE SERMON

AFFIRMATION OF FAITH

Let us proclaim our faith in God.

Do you believe and trust in God the Father, source of all being and life, the one for whom we exist?
We believe and trust in him.

Do you believe and trust in God the Son who took our human nature, died for us, and rose again?
We believe and trust in him.

Do you believe and trust in God the Holy Spirit, who gives life to the people of God and makes Christ known in the world?
We believe and trust in him.

This is the faith of the Church.
This is our faith.
We believe and trust in one God,
Father, Son and Holy Spirit. **Amen.**

(A HYMN may be sung)

The Prayers

INTERCESSIONS

(Special thanksgivings and prayers ...)

Friends and followers of Jesus, we have come together because of his love for us and our faith in him. Let us now pray for all who need the strength and guidance of God's Spirit in meeting the challenges that life brings.

For bishop N. and for all Church ministers, clergy and lay, that they will serve in humility and holiness ...
Jesus, Lord and Saviour,
(R:) send the Holy Spirit upon us.

For our Queen and government and the leaders of other nations, that they will promote peace and justice, freedom and opportunity ...
Jesus, Lord and Saviour, **(R:)**

For those places in the world where food is scarce, jobs are few or life is dangerous, that the strong will help the weak in their struggle for a better life ...
Jesus, Lord and Saviour, **(R:)**

For the needy and vulnerable in our own neighbourhood, that we may respond to their plight with compassion and practical care ...
Jesus, Lord and Saviour, **(R:)**

For our families and all who are close to us, that in times of trial they will be protected from harm and make the right choices ...
Jesus, Lord and Saviour, **(R:)**

For all who face disability or chronic illness, that they may have encouragement in coping with their difficulties ...
Jesus, Lord and Saviour, **(R:)**

For those who are ill, in pain, or undergoing treatment, that they will be healed and restored to a better quality of life ...
Jesus, Lord and Saviour, **(R:)**

For those in darkness and grief because they are parted from someone they love, that they will be comforted, and lifted by hope ...
Jesus, Lord and Saviour, **answer all the prayers we offer according to your will.**
Amen.

THE LORD'S PRAYER

(A HYMN may be sung)

CONCLUDING PRAYER

God be in my head
and in my understanding.
God be in my eyes and in my looking.
God be in my mouth and in my speaking.
God be in my heart and in my thinking.
God be at mine end
and at my departing. *(St Patrick)*

(THE BLESSING or THE GRACE is said)

THE THIRTEENTH SUNDAY AFTER TRINITY
'Proclaim the good news of God's love'

The gospel (or 'good news') is that God in Christ has reconciled lost human beings to himself. He sent his Son to seek them out, offer them love and forgiveness, and bring them under the rule of God. In this Kingdom they are reconciled to their heavenly Father, and to each other, and are sent on a mission: to be agents of reconciliation in a divided world.

The Gathering

THE GREETING
Grace, mercy and peace from God our Father and the Lord Jesus Christ be with you.
And also with you. *(1 Tim. 1:2)*

(A HYMN may be sung)

If anyone is in Christ, there is a new creation.
Everything old has passed away;
See, everything has become new!
All this is from God,
who reconciled us to himself through Christ.
We entreat you on behalf of Christ,
be reconciled to God. *(2 Cor. 5:17ff)*

PRAYER
God our Father,
we thank you that we are no longer strangers to you but members together in the body of Christ.
Send the Holy Spirit
to build up our unity,
inspire our worship,
and lead us on in the service
of Jesus Christ, our Lord.
Amen.

(SONGS may be sung)

* * * * *

PENITENCE
Jesus said, 'Before you offer your gift, go and be reconciled.'
Let us, in a moment of silence, recognize those failings in us that undermine relationships, and cause hurt to others …
As brothers and sisters in God's family, we come together to ask our Father for forgiveness:
We confess the sins that bring hurt and betrayal upon those who trust us.
Lord, have mercy.
We confess the sins that cause love to grow cold, and attitudes to harden.
Christ, have mercy.
We confess the sins that impede the way to forgiveness and reconciliation.
Lord, have mercy.

God, the Father of mercies, has reconciled the world to himself through the death and resurrection of his Son, Jesus Christ, not counting our trespasses against us, but sending his Holy Spirit
to shed abroad his love among us.
By the ministry of reconciliation
entrusted by Christ to his Church,
receive his pardon and peace
to stand before him in his strength alone,
this day and evermore. **Amen.**

(The GLORIA, the VENITE, a SONG or RESPONSES may be used)

THE COLLECT OF THE DAY
Let us pray … *(silent prayer)*

Almighty God, who called your Church to bear witness that you were in Christ reconciling the world to yourself: help us to proclaim the good news of your love, that all who hear it may be drawn to you; through him who was lifted up on the cross, and reigns with you in the unity of the Holy Spirit, one God, now and for ever. **Amen.**

The Liturgy of the Word

THE SCRIPTURE READING(S)

(After the reading)
This is the Word of the Lord.
Thanks be to God.

PSALM/HYMN or SCRIPTURAL SONG

THE GOSPEL

Hear the Gospel of our Lord Jesus Christ according to N.
Glory to you, O Lord.

(After the reading)
This is the Gospel of the Lord.
Praise to you, O Christ.

THE SERMON

AFFIRMATION OF FAITH

I believe in God, the Father almighty,
creator of heaven and earth
I believe in Jesus Christ,
his only Son, our Lord, who was
conceived by the Holy Spirit,
born of the Virgin Mary,
suffered under Pontius Pilate,
was crucified, died, and was buried;
he descended to the dead.
On the third day he rose again;
he ascended into heaven,
he is seated at the right hand of the
Father, and he will come
to judge the living and the dead.
I believe in the Holy Spirit,
the holy catholic Church,
the communion of saints,
the forgiveness of sins,
the resurrection of the body,
and the life everlasting. **Amen.**
(The Apostles' Creed)

(A HYMN may be sung)

The Prayers

INTERCESSIONS

(Special thanksgivings and prayers …)

Our Father in heaven, we give thanks for the Church and for all that we receive through its worship, teaching and fellowship. We pray for bishop N. and the life of this diocese … For each other here and all who minister among us … For our fellow Christians in other places … Renew us by the Holy Spirit that we may grow as disciples of Christ.
Lord God, **hear our prayer.**

We give thanks for this nation and those in authority who serve the people with integrity and dedication. We pray:
for our Queen and government … For all who shape our culture, especially those working in the media … For people anywhere suffering from disaster, war or oppression … Bring justice to all, and the opportunity to make the most of their lives.
Lord God, **hear our prayer.**

We give thanks for our community, and for those who cherish us. Strengthen the bonds of trust between husbands and wives, parents and children, friends and neighbours …
Lord God, **hear our prayer.**

We give thanks for the health we have, and for the skills of those who attend to us when we are in need. Bring healing and encouragement to those suffering from ill-health, depression or frailty …
Lord God, **hear our prayer.**

We give thanks for those whose memory we treasure …
Grant us with them, and with all the saints … the joy of eternal life
in Christ our Lord. **Amen.**

THE LORD'S PRAYER

(A HYMN may be sung)

CONCLUDING PRAYER

May the grace of Christ our Saviour,
and the Father's boundless love,
with the Holy Spirit's favour,
rest upon us from above.

Thus may we abide in union
with each other and the Lord,
and possess, in sweet communion,
joys which earth cannot afford. **Amen.**
(J. Newton)

(The BLESSING may be said)

THE FOURTEENTH SUNDAY AFTER TRINITY
'Worship in spirit and in truth'

Today's Collect, quoting Jesus' words in John 4:24, asks God to help us worship him 'in spirit and in truth'. This means celebrating God's love for his world, within a true and spiritual relationship to him as the Father – not within an old, rigid tradition. This new, living relationship has been opened up for us by Jesus Christ. We come to the Father only through him.

The Gathering

THE GREETING
The Lord be with you.
And also with you.

(A HYMN may be sung)

O Lord, open my lips:
and my mouth will declare your praise.
(Ps. 51:15)

Jesus said: 'God is spirit,
and those who worship him must worship in spirit and truth.' *(John 4:24)*

St Paul wrote:
'Sing psalms, hymns and spiritual songs to God: do everything in the name of the Lord Jesus,
giving thanks to God the Father through him.' *(Col. 3:16-17ff)*

PRAYER
Almighty God,
to whom all hearts are open,
all desires known,
and from whom no secrets are hidden:
cleanse the thoughts of our hearts
by the inspiration of your Holy Spirit,
that we may perfectly love you,
and worthily magnify your holy name;
through Christ our Lord. **Amen.**

(SONGS may be sung)
* * * * *

PENITENCE
We have gathered here to worship God, conscious of our unworthiness to do so. Using words of St Augustine, we pray:

Lord Jesus, our Saviour, let us come near.

Our hearts are cold, **Lord have mercy.**
Warm them with your selfless love.

Our hearts are sinful, **Christ have mercy.**
Cleanse them with your precious blood.

Our hearts are weak, **Lord have mercy.**
Strengthen them with your joyous Spirit.

Our hearts are empty, **Christ have mercy.**
Fill them with your divine presence.

Lord Jesus, our hearts are yours,
possess them always and only for yourself. **Amen.**

May almighty God have mercy on *us*,
forgive *us* our sins,
and bring *us* to everlasting life,
through Jesus Christ our Lord. **Amen.**

(The GLORIA, the VENITE, a SONG or RESPONSES may be used)

THE COLLECT OF THE DAY
Let us pray ... *(silent prayer)*

Almighty God, whose only Son has opened for us a new and living way into your presence: give us pure hearts and steadfast wills to worship you in spirit and in truth; through Jesus Christ your Son our Lord, who is alive and reigns with you, in the unity of the Holy Spirit one God, now and for ever. **Amen.**

The Liturgy of the Word

THE SCRIPTURE READING(S)

(After the reading)
This is the Word of the Lord.
Thanks be to God.

PSALM/HYMN or SCRIPTURAL SONG

THE GOSPEL
Hear the Gospel of our Lord Jesus Christ according to N.
Glory to you, O Lord.

(After the reading)
This is the Gospel of the Lord.
Praise to you, O Christ.

THE SERMON

AFFIRMATION OF FAITH
Let us affirm our faith in God:

Do you believe and trust in God the Father, source of all being and life, the one for whom we exist?
We believe and trust in him.

Do you believe and trust in God the Son who took our human nature, died for us, and rose again?
We believe and trust in him.

Do you believe and trust in God the Holy Spirit, who gives life to the people of God and makes Christ known in the world?
We believe and trust in him.

This is the faith of the Church.
This is our faith.
We believe and trust in one God,
Father, Son and Holy Spirit.   Amen.

(A HYMN may be sung)

The Prayers

INTERCESSIONS
(Special thanksgivings and prayers ...)

Father God, who knows our needs before we ask, hear our prayers for all people:

Give grace to those who minister in your Church: Bishop N., the clergy and all lay ministers ... Anoint them with the Holy Spirit for their work in building up the body of Christ.
Lord, in your mercy,   ***hear our prayer.***

Sustain our Christian brothers and sisters in other places who are persecuted ... Deliver those who are in prison for their beliefs.
Lord, in your mercy,   ***hear our prayer.***

Guide our Queen and government and the leaders of the nations in all their decisions ... Bring reconciliation to situations where there is deep and bitter conflict, and new opportunities for all to make the most of their lives.
Lord, in your mercy,   ***hear our prayer.***

Enlighten all who are engaged in scientific research. May their work promote the life, health and well-being of the world.
Lord, in your mercy,   ***hear our prayer.***

Bless the work of our local schools ... Give teachers the skill, enthusiasm and patience to inspire the young to learn.
Lord, in your mercy,   ***hear our prayer.***

Be with those whose work is very demanding or unrewarding ... Give employers understanding of their needs.
Lord, in your mercy,   ***hear our prayer.***

Be close to those who are unwell, frail or disabled ... Bless all who bring healing and care, and who sustain hope.
Lord, in your mercy,   ***hear our prayer.***

We remember with thanksgiving those who have died ... Strengthen all who grieve, with comfort, faith and peace, for Jesus' sake.
Amen.

THE LORD'S PRAYER

(A HYMN may be sung)

CONCLUDING PRAYER
In our hearts and homes
we pray for the love of God the Father.
In our living and caring
we pray for the grace of God the Son.
In our coming and going
we pray for the power of God the Holy Spirit.   Amen.

(THE BLESSING or THE GRACE is said)

THE FIFTEENTH SUNDAY AFTER TRINITY
'Fervent in the fellowship of the Gospel'

The 'fellowship of the Gospel' to which the Collect refers, is a phrase taken from St Paul's letter to the Philippians (1:5) in which he applauds the way they have shared in the great mission to proclaim everywhere the gospel (good news) of salvation in Christ. Today we pray that the Holy Spirit will continue to equip God's people for this mission, making them 'fervent' in faith and love.

The Gathering

THE GREETING
The grace and mercy of our Lord Jesus Christ be with you.
And also with you.

(A HYMN may be sung)

Rejoice in the Lord always;
again I will say, Rejoice.

Let your gentleness be known to everyone.
The Lord is near.

Do not worry about anything, but in everything by prayer and supplication with thanksgiving
let your requests be made known to God.

And the peace of God which surpasses all understanding
will guard your hearts and your minds in Christ Jesus.   *(Phil. 4:4-7)*

PRAYER
Heavenly Father,
in our time together now, help us
to celebrate your love,
learn from your truth, trust in your grace
and grow strong in your service
through Jesus Christ our Lord.   **Amen.**

(SONGS may be sung)
* * * * *

PENITENCE
Jesus' Summary of the Law
(Mark 12:29-31)
The first commandment is:
'You shall love the Lord your God with all your heart, and with all your soul, and with all your mind, and with all your strength.'
The second is this:
'You shall love your neighbour as yourself.'

Let us confess to God our failure truly to serve him and our neighbour.

Most merciful God,
Father of our Lord Jesus Christ,
we confess that we have sinned
in thought, word and deed.
We have not loved you with our whole heart. We have not loved our neighbours as ourselves.
In your mercy forgive what we have been,
help us to amend what we are,
and direct what we shall be;
that we may do justly, love mercy,
and walk humbly with you, our God.
                                    Amen.

May almighty God have mercy on *us*,
forgive *us* *our* sins,
and bring *us* to everlasting life,
through Jesus Christ our Lord.   **Amen.**

(The GLORIA, the VENITE, a SONG or RESPONSES may be used)

THE COLLECT OF THE DAY
Let us pray …   *(silent prayer)*

God, who in generous mercy sent the Holy Spirit upon your Church in the burning fire of your love: grant that your people may be fervent in the fellowship of the gospel that, always abiding in you, they may be found steadfast in faith and active in service; through Jesus Christ your Son our Lord, who is alive and reigns with you, in the unity of the Holy Spirit, one God, now and for ever.   **Amen.**

The Liturgy of the Word

THE SCRIPTURE READING(S)

(After the reading)
This is the Word of the Lord.
Thanks be to God.

PSALM/HYMN or SCRIPTURAL SONG

THE GOSPEL
Hear the Gospel of our Lord Jesus Christ according to N.
Glory to you, O Lord.

(After the reading)
This is the Gospel of the Lord.
Praise to you, O Christ.

THE SERMON

AFFIRMATION OF FAITH
Let us affirm our faith in God:

**We believe in God the Father,
from whom every family
in heaven and on earth is named.**

**We believe in God the Son,
who lives in our hearts through faith,
and fills us with his love.**

**We believe in God the Holy Spirit,
who strengthens us
with power from on high.**

**We believe in one God;
Father, Son and Holy Spirit. Amen.**
(from Eph. 3)

(A HYMN may be sung)

The Prayers

INTERCESSIONS
(Special thanksgivings and prayers …)

We bring to you, Father God, the needs of all people, for whose salvation you sent your Son Jesus Christ:

We pray for our Queen and government, and the leaders of the nations … We think of people divided by national enmity, religious intolerance, or racial prejudice …
Lord Jesus, where there is hatred,
let me sow love.

We pray for husbands and wives, parents and children, employers and employees … We think of families, communities and work places where relationships have broken down …
Lord Jesus, where there is injury,
let me sow pardon.

We pray for bishop N., for all who teach the Christian faith, and for the life of our church … We think of those whose faith is being sorely tested …
Lord Jesus, where there is doubt,
let me sow faith.

We remember with thanksgiving those who have died … We think of all who are overshadowed by loss or loneliness … We pray for all in need … We pray for their families and friends, doctors, nurses and carers.
Lord Jesus, where there is despair,
let me give hope.

We think of ourselves, our self-centredness, our faltering attempts to serve you …
Lord Jesus,
***make us channels of your peace
and witnesses of your Kingdom. Amen.***

THE LORD'S PRAYER

(A HYMN may be sung)

CONCLUDING PRAYER
***May the God of hope fill us
with all joy and peace in believing,
through the power of the Holy Spirit.
Amen.*** *(Rom. 15:13)*

(THE BLESSING or THE GRACE is said)

THE SIXTEENTH SUNDAY AFTER TRINITY
'Knowing what we ought to do'

Today's Collect reminds us that prayer is more than simply asking God for something and waiting for an answer. We are part of the answer, for God works through us. We ask him what things we ought to **do**, and pray for grace and power to carry them out. As someone once said: 'Pray as if everything depended on God. Do as if everything depended on you.'

The Gathering

THE GREETING
Grace, mercy and peace from God our Father and the Lord Jesus Christ be with you.
And also with you. *(1 Tim. 1:2)*

(A HYMN may be sung)

Praise the Lord!
O give thanks to the Lord, for he is good;
for his steadfast love endures for ever.

Save us, O Lord our God,
and gather us from among the nations,
that we may give thanks to your holy name
and glory in your praise.

Blessed be the Lord, the God of Israel,
from everlasting to everlasting.

And let all the people say,
'Amen. Praise the Lord!'
(Ps. 106:1-2, 47-48)

PRAYER
**God our Father,
we are here to worship you
and learn more of your love for us
through Jesus Christ.
Renew us by your Spirit
that we may grow
in faith, hope and love,
for Jesus' sake.** **Amen.**

(SONGS may be sung)

* * * * *

PENITENCE
We reflect silently, in the presence of our holy and merciful God, where our lives have gone wrong, and where we have failed to live up to the Christian values we profess ...
(silence)
Let us confess our sins and shortcomings:

Gracious God,
we pretend to be good when we are not ...
How quick we are to find fault in others.
Lord, have mercy. **Lord, have mercy.**

Merciful Lord,
we turn our backs on those who need us ...
How slow we are to do good.
Christ, have mercy. **Christ, have mercy.**

Holy God,
we place our own interests above everything else ...
How reluctant we are to seek your will.
Lord, have mercy, **Lord, have mercy.**

May almighty God have mercy on *us*,
forgive *us our* sins,
and bring *us* to everlasting life,
through Jesus Christ our Lord. **Amen.**

(The GLORIA, the VENITE, a SONG or RESPONSES may be used)

THE COLLECT OF THE DAY
Let us pray ... *(silent prayer)*

O Lord,
we beseech you mercifully
to hear the prayers of your people
who call upon you;
and grant that they may both perceive
and know what things they ought to do,
and also may have grace and power
faithfully to fulfil them;
through Jesus Christ your Son our Lord,
who is alive and reigns with you,
in the unity of the Holy Spirit,
one God, now and for ever. **Amen.**

The Liturgy of the Word

THE SCRIPTURE READING(S)

(After the reading)
This is the Word of the Lord.
Thanks be to God.

PSALM/HYMN or SCRIPTURAL SONG

THE GOSPEL
Hear the Gospel of our Lord Jesus Christ according to N.
Glory to you, O Lord.

(After the reading)
This is the Gospel of the Lord.
Praise to you, O Christ.

THE SERMON

AFFIRMATION OF FAITH
We affirm our faith in God:

Do you believe and trust in God the Father, source of all being and life, the one for whom we exist?
We believe and trust in him.

Do you believe and trust in God the Son who took our human nature, died for us, and rose again?
We believe and trust in him.

Do you believe and trust in God the Holy Spirit who gives life to the people of God and makes Christ known in the world?
We believe and trust in him.

This is the faith of the Church.
This is our faith.
We believe and trust in one God,
Father, Son and Holy Spirit. Amen.

(A HYMN may be sung)

The Prayers

INTERCESSIONS
(Special thanksgivings and prayers ...)

Our Father in heaven, we pray for all people, in the name of your Son Jesus Christ:

We pray for the Church, for bishop N., and for all who lead, teach and minister in Christ's name ... Grant that we may be nourished in our faith and understanding, and bear daily witness to Christ's love.
Lord of life, **in your mercy, hear us.**

We pray for the nations of the world and for those who take authority to serve the cause of justice and human well-being ... Strengthen our Queen and the leaders of the nations with gifts of wisdom, courage and integrity, that your will may be done on earth as it is in heaven.
Lord of life, **in your mercy, hear us.**

We pray for those who are afflicted by natural disasters, or caught up in brutal conflicts ...
Fill them with the resurrection hope that good will prevail, and bless all who stand with them in finding solutions to their difficulties.
Lord of life, **in your mercy, hear us.**

We pray for the people we are called to serve, in the home, the neighbourhood and at work ... Help us to work hard at building good relationships, and to strive for reconciliation when they break down.
Lord of life, **in your mercy, hear us.**

We pray for all who suffer from illness, loneliness or loss ... Raise them from despair to hopefulness and health.
Lord of life, **in your mercy, hear us.**

We remember with thanksgiving those who have died ... Strengthen all who mourn, with the sure hope that, in Christ, their loved ones are raised to fullness of life.
Lord of life, **in your mercy, hear us.**

Accept all these prayers
for the sake of your Son
our Saviour Jesus Christ. Amen.

THE LORD'S PRAYER

(A HYMN may be sung)

CONCLUDING PRAYER
Teach me my God and King
in all things thee to see,
and what I do in anything
to do it as for thee. Amen.
(George Herbert)

(The BLESSING or the GRACE is said)

THE SEVENTEENTH SUNDAY AFTER TRINITY

'Hearts are restless till they find their rest in God'

Today's Collect, quoting from a prayer of St Augustine (a North African bishop who died in 430 AD), refers to the relationship all human beings have with their Creator, who has 'made us for yourself'. However, when we become disconnected from God our hearts grow 'restless' and seek satisfaction in the wrong things. Pray that we will grow in the knowledge of God's love and find our eternal home in him.

The Gathering

THE GREETING
May the light and peace of Jesus Christ our Lord be with you.
The Lord bless you.

(A HYMN may be sung)

As a deer longs for flowing streams,
so my soul longs for you, O God.
***My soul thirsts for God,
for the living God.***
Hope in God,
***for I shall again praise him,
my help and my God.***
(Ps. 42:1-2, 5)

PRAYER
***Almighty God,
to whom all hearts are open,
all desires known,
and from whom no secrets are hidden:
cleanse the thoughts of our hearts
by the inspiration of your Holy Spirit,
that we may perfectly love you,
and worthily magnify your holy name;
through Christ our Lord.   Amen.***

(SONGS may be sung)

* * * * *

PENITENCE
We have gathered here to worship God, but are conscious of our unworthiness to do so. Jesus challenged the hypocrisy of people who 'honour God with their lips but their hearts are far from him.'   *(Mark 7:6)*

Let us confess our sins to Almighty God, in penitence and faith:

When we devote much attention to satisfying our bodies but little to satisfying our souls ...
Lord, have mercy.   ***Lord, have mercy.***

When we like to be regarded as followers of Jesus but avoid making any sacrifices for him ...
Christ, have mercy.   ***Christ, have mercy.***

When we say we love God but fail to care for our brothers and sisters in need ...
Lord, have mercy.   ***Lord, have mercy.***

Almighty God,
who forgives all who truly repent,
have mercy upon *us,*
pardon and deliver *us* from all *our* sins,
confirm and strengthen *us* in all goodness,
and keep *us* in life eternal;
through Jesus Christ our Lord.   **Amen.**

(The GLORIA, the VENITE, a SONG or RESPONSES may be used)

THE COLLECT OF THE DAY
Let us pray ...   *(silent prayer)*
Almighty God,
you have made us for yourself, and our hearts are restless till they find their rest in you: pour your love into our hearts and draw us to yourself, and so bring us at last to your heavenly city where we shall see you face to face;
through Jesus Christ your Son our Lord,
who is alive and reigns with you,
in the unity of the Holy Spirit,
one God, now and for ever.   **Amen.**

The Liturgy of the Word

THE SCRIPTURE READING(S)

(After the reading)
This is the Word of the Lord.
Thanks be to God.

PSALM/HYMN or SCRIPTURAL SONG

THE GOSPEL

Hear the Gospel of our Lord Jesus Christ according to N.
Glory to you, O Lord.

(After the reading)
This is the Gospel of the Lord.
Praise to you, O Christ.

THE SERMON

AFFIRMATION OF FAITH

Let us declare our faith in God:

Do you believe and trust in God the Father, source of all being and life, the one for whom we exist?
We believe and trust in him.

Do you believe and trust in God the Son who took our human nature, died for us, and rose again?
We believe and trust in him.

Do you believe and trust in God the Holy Spirit who gives life to the people of God and makes Christ known in the world?
We believe and trust in him.

This is the faith of the Church.
This is our faith.
We believe and trust in one God,
Father, Son and Holy Spirit. Amen.

(A HYMN may be sung)

The Prayers

INTERCESSIONS

(Special thanksgivings and prayers …)

Father God, we pray for the world, starved of compassion and forgiveness …
Father, hear our prayer
(R:) and grant us your Spirit.

For the Church, whose witness is often weakened by disunity …
We pray for bishop N., and all ministers and people, that our life together may bring honour to Christ.
Father, hear our prayer **(R:)**

For all situations of violence, hostility and racial prejudice … We pray for our leaders, and for peace and justice between nations and within communities.
Father, hear our prayer **(R:)**

For all families struggling in the face of poverty, disadvantage or disability … We pray that they will have encouragement and support to find a way through their troubles.
Father, hear our prayer **(R:)**

For the lonely and the isolated, the rejected and the long-term unemployed … We pray that we will not forget them.
Father, hear our prayer **(R:)**

For those who have died, especially …
We pray for their loved ones left behind that comfort and hope will lessen their sorrows.
Father, hear our prayer **(R:)**

For all who are burdened by worry, ill-health or pain … We pray that they will know relief and healing, through those who care.
Father, hear our prayer **(R:)**

We remember with joy your unfailing love, and pray that we may show our thanks not only with our lips but in our lives.
Hear, O Lord, **and answer all our prayers through Jesus Christ our Lord.** Amen.

THE LORD'S PRAYER

(A HYMN may be sung)

CONCLUDING PRAYER

Almighty God, give us
wisdom to perceive you,
intellect to understand you,
diligence to seek you,
patience to wait for you,
a vision to meditate upon you,
and a life to proclaim you. Amen

(St Benedict)
(THE BLESSING or THE GRACE is said)

THE EIGHTEENTH SUNDAY AFTER TRINITY
'Running the way of God's commandments'

Using the image of life as a race; today's Collect asks God to help us: *'forsake what lies behind'* – **travel light**, freed by Jesus from the weight of past sins;
'reach out to that which is before' – **travel in hope**, longing for God's Kingdom to come;
'run the way of God's commandments' – **travel straight**, following Jesus, and *'win the crown of everlasting joy'*.

The Gathering

THE GREETING
Grace, mercy and peace from God our Father and the Lord Jesus Christ be with you.
And also with you. *(1 Tim. 1:2)*

(A HYMN may be sung)

St Paul wrote these words to the church at Philippi:
Beloved, this one thing I do:
forgetting what lies behind and
straining forward to what lies ahead,
I press on toward the goal for the prize of the heavenly call of God in Christ Jesus.
Let us hold fast to what we have attained. *(Phil. 3:13-14, 16)*

PRAYER
**Father God,
as we journey home to you,
and face the changes and challenges of life on the way,
send your Holy Spirit among us now
that together we may grow
in faith, hope and love,
united to him who is The Way,
Jesus Christ our Lord.** **Amen.**

(SONGS may be sung)

* * * * *

PENITENCE
Since we are surrounded by so great a cloud of witnesses, let us lay aside every weight, and the sin that clings so closely, and let us run with perseverance the race that is set before us, looking to Jesus the pioneer and perfecter of our faith …. *(Heb. 12:1-2)*

We confess our sins to God in penitence and faith, saying:
**Almighty God, our heavenly Father,
we have sinned against you
and against our neighbour,
in thought and word and deed,
through negligence, through weakness,
through our own deliberate fault.
We are truly sorry
and repent of all our sins.
For the sake of your Son Jesus Christ,
who died for us,
forgive us all that is past;
and grant that we may serve you
in newness of life
to the glory of your name.** **Amen.**

May almighty God have mercy on *us*,
forgive *us our* sins,
and bring *us* to everlasting life,
through Jesus Christ our Lord. **Amen.**

(The GLORIA, the VENITE, a SONG or RESPONSES may be used)

THE COLLECT OF THE DAY
Let us pray … *(silent prayer)*

Almighty and everlasting God,
increase in us your gift of faith
that, forsaking what lies behind
and reaching out to that which is before;
we may run the way of your commandments
and win the crown of everlasting joy;
through Jesus Christ your Son our Lord,
who is alive and reigns with you,
in the unity of the Holy Spirit,
one God, now and for ever. **Amen.**

The Liturgy of the Word

THE SCRIPTURE READING(S)

(After the reading)
This is the Word of the Lord.
Thanks be to God.

PSALM/HYMN or SCRIPTURAL SONG

THE GOSPEL

Hear the Gospel of our Lord Jesus Christ according to N.
Glory to you, O Lord.

(After the reading)
This is the Gospel of the Lord.
Praise to you, O Christ.

THE SERMON

AFFIRMATION OF FAITH

Let us declare our faith in God:

I believe in God, the Father almighty, creator of heaven and earth.
I believe in Jesus Christ,
his only Son, our Lord, who was conceived by the Holy Spirit, born of the Virgin Mary, suffered under Pontius Pilate, was crucified, died, and was buried;
he descended to the dead.
On the third day he rose again;
he ascended into heaven,
he is seated at the right hand of the Father, and he will come
to judge the living and the dead.

I believe in the Holy Spirit,
the holy catholic Church, the communion of saints, the forgiveness of sins, the resurrection of the body, and the life everlasting. Amen.

(The Apostles' Creed)

(A HYMN may be sung)

The Prayers

INTERCESSIONS

(Special thanksgivings and prayers ...)

Father God, we pray for your holy catholic apostolic Church;
that all may be one in Christ, our risen Saviour.

Grant that every member of the Church may grow in knowledge of you, and faithfully serve you;
that your Kingdom may come and your will be done.

We pray for bishop N., all clergy and lay workers;
that they may be faithful ministers of your truth and grace.

We pray for our Queen and all who hold authority in the nations of the world;
that there may be justice and peace on the earth.

Give us grace to do your will in all that we plan and do;
that our works may bring glory to your Name.

Fill us with compassion for those who suffer from any grief, trouble or injustice;
that they may be delivered from distress.

We remember with thanksgiving those who have died ... We praise you for your saints who have entered into eternal rest;
may we also come to share in your eternal joy.

In a moment of silence, let us pray for those we most deeply care about ...
Merciful Father,
accept all these prayers for the sake of your Son our Saviour Jesus Christ.
Amen.

THE LORD'S PRAYER

(A HYMN may be sung)

CONCLUDING PRAYER

**Lord, be thou a bright flame before me.
Be thou a guiding star above me.
Be thou a smooth path below me.
Be thou a kindly shepherd behind me.
Today – tonight – and forever. Amen.**

(St Columba)

(THE BLESSING or THE GRACE is said)

THE NINETEENTH SUNDAY AFTER TRINITY
'May the Holy Spirit … direct and rule our hearts'

Of all the blessings that God gives to his people, the most vital is the gift of the Holy Spirit. Jesus taught that the Father longs to give him to those who ask (Luke 11:13). The Spirit endows us with gifts of energy, love and knowledge of Christ and, as today's Collect puts it, 'directs and rules our hearts'. Let us keep asking our Father for the life-giving Spirit.

The Gathering

THE GREETING
May the light and peace of Jesus Christ our Lord be with you.
The Lord bless you.

(A HYMN may be sung)

Jesus said: Ask, and it will be given you;
search, and you will find;
knock, and the door will be opened for you.
For everyone who asks receives,
and everyone who searches finds,
and for everyone who knocks,
the door will be opened.
If you know how to give good gifts to your children,
how much more will the heavenly Father give the Holy Spirit to those who ask him!
(Luke 11:9-10, 13)

PRAYER
Almighty God, to whom
all hearts are open, all desires known,
and from whom no secrets are hidden:
cleanse the thoughts of our hearts
by the inspiration of your Holy Spirit,
that we may perfectly love you,
and worthily magnify your holy name;
through Christ our Lord. **Amen.**

(SONGS may be sung)

* * * * *

PENITENCE
In the presence of our holy and merciful Lord, we measure our Christian lives against the nine-fold fruits listed by St Paul.
(Gal. 5:22-23)

'The fruit of the Spirit is love, joy and peace.'
Forgive us, Lord, when we have pursued our own interests rather than the things that make for peace.
Lord, have mercy. **Lord, have mercy.**

'The fruit of the Spirit is patience, kindness and generosity.'
Forgive us, Lord, when we have been intolerant of other people's failings, or uncaring about their needs.
Christ, have mercy. **Christ, have mercy.**

'The fruit of the spirit is faithfulness, gentleness and self-control.'
Forgive us, Lord, when we have let people down, or failed to place our trust in you.
Lord, have mercy. **Lord, have mercy.**

May almighty God have mercy on *us*,
forgive *us our* sins,
and bring *us* to everlasting life,
through Jesus Christ our Lord. **Amen.**

(The GLORIA, the VENITE, a SONG or RESPONSES may be used)

THE COLLECT OF THE DAY
Let us pray … *(silent prayer)*

O God, forasmuch as without you
we are not able to please you;
mercifully grant that your Holy Spirit
may in all things direct and rule our hearts;
through Jesus Christ your Son our Lord,
who is alive and reigns with you,
in the unity of the Holy Spirit,
one God, now and for ever. **Amen.**

The Liturgy of the Word

THE SCRIPTURE READING(S)

(After the reading)
This is the Word of the Lord.
Thanks be to God.

PSALM/HYMN or SCRIPTURAL SONG

THE GOSPEL
Hear the Gospel of our Lord Jesus Christ according to N.
Glory to you, O Lord.

(After the reading)
This is the Gospel of the Lord.
Praise to you, O Christ.

THE SERMON

AFFIRMATION OF FAITH
We affirm our faith in God:

Do you believe and trust in God the Father, who made all things?
We believe and trust in him.

Do you believe and trust in his Son Jesus Christ, who redeemed the world?
We believe and trust in him.

Do you believe and trust in his Holy Spirit, who gives life to the people of God?
We believe and trust in him.

This is the faith of the Church.
This is our faith.
We believe and trust in one God,
Father, Son and Holy Spirit. Amen.

(A HYMN may be sung)

The Prayers

INTERCESSIONS
(Special thanksgivings and prayers …)

Our Father in heaven, we bring you our prayers for the church and for all people. Send your Holy Spirit to equip them with the gifts that are needed to serve you:

For our bishop N. and all ministers of God's word and sacraments, that they may serve your church in love, and build up your people in truth and faith …
Let us pray to the Lord. **Lord, hear us.**

For the peace and well-being of the world, for our Queen and the leaders of the nations and for the resolution of deep and bitter conflicts …
Let us pray to the Lord. **Lord, hear us.**

For the innocent victims of violence or injustice, and for all who strive to overcome evil with good …
Let us pray to the Lord. **Lord, hear us.**

For our families and those close to us, and for all who need our time, our attention and our care …
Let us pray to the Lord. **Lord, hear us.**

For the sick, the suffering, the sorrowful and the dying, and for all who bring healing and hope to them …
Let us pray to the Lord. **Lord, hear us.**

We remember with thanksgiving those who have died …
Father of all, **grant us with them and all the saints, a share in your eternal kingdom, through Jesus Christ our Lord.**
Amen.

THE LORD'S PRAYER

(A HYMN may be sung)

CONCLUDING PRAYER
Almighty and everlasting Father,
we thank you that you have brought us
safely to the beginning of this day.
Keep us from falling into sin
or running into danger;
order us in all our doings;
and guide us to do always
what is right in your eyes;
through Jesus Christ our Lord. Amen.
(Collect from Common Worship)

(THE BLESSING or THE GRACE is said)

THE TWENTIETH SUNDAY AFTER TRINITY
'Eager to do God's will'

Like water from an underground spring that gives life to the plants nearby, the Holy Spirit of God – in the words of today's Collect – 'wells up within the Church' to bring life to God's people. He equips them with all the gifts they need 'to live the gospel of Christ', makes them 'eager to do God's will', and enables them to share in 'the joys of eternal life'.

The Gathering

THE GREETING
Grace, mercy and peace from God
our Father and the Lord Jesus Christ
be with you.   *(1 Tim. 1:2)*
And also with you.

The Lord is here.
His Spirit is with us.

(A HYMN may be sung)

I will bless the Lord at all times;
his praise shall continually be in my mouth.
O magnify the Lord with me,
and let us exalt his name together.
O taste and see that the Lord is good;
happy are those who take refuge in him.
(Ps. 34:1, 3, 8)

PRAYER
Almighty God, to whom
all hearts are open, all desires known,
and from whom no secrets are hidden:
cleanse the thoughts of our hearts
by the inspiration of your Holy Spirit,
that we may perfectly love you,
and worthily magnify your holy name;
through Christ our Lord.   **Amen.**

(SONGS may be sung)

* * * * *

PENITENCE
In God's holy presence let us examine the words of our mouths, the deeds of our bodies, and the desires of our minds, confessing our sins to him …

When we are quick to criticize others, but slow to praise them …
Lord, have mercy.   **Lord, have mercy.**

When we bear grudges, and find it hard to forgive …
Christ, have mercy.   **Christ, have mercy.**

When we think we are right, and impose our views on others …
Lord, have mercy.   **Lord, have mercy.**

When we let evil go unchallenged, and are afraid to speak the truth …
Christ, have mercy.   **Christ, have mercy.**

When we are preoccupied with ourselves, and give little attention to others …
Lord, have mercy.   **Lord, have mercy.**

When we trust in material things, more than in God's unfailing love …
Christ, have mercy.   **Christ, have mercy.**

May almighty God have mercy on *us*,
forgive *us* our sins,
and bring *us* to everlasting life,
through Jesus Christ our Lord.   **Amen.**

(The GLORIA, the VENITE, a SONG or RESPONSES may be used)

THE COLLECT OF THE DAY
Let us pray …   *(silent prayer)*

God, the giver of life,
whose Holy Spirit wells up within your Church: by the Spirit's gifts
equip us to live the gospel of Christ
and make us eager to do your will,
that we may share with the whole creation
the joys of eternal life;
through Jesus Christ your Son our Lord,
who is alive and reigns with you,
in the unity of the Holy Spirit,
one God, now and for ever.   **Amen.**

The Liturgy of the Word

THE SCRIPTURE READING(S)

(After the reading)
This is the Word of the Lord.
Thanks be to God.

PSALM/HYMN or SCRIPTURAL SONG

THE GOSPEL
Hear the Gospel of our Lord Jesus Christ according to N.
Glory to you, O Lord.

(After the reading)
This is the Gospel of the Lord.
Praise to you, O Christ.

THE SERMON

AFFIRMATION OF FAITH
Let us declare our faith in God:

We believe in God the Father,
from whom every family
in heaven and on earth is named.

We believe in God the Son,
who lives in our hearts through faith
and fills us with his love.

We believe in God the Holy Spirit,
who strengthens us
with power from on high.

We believe in one God;
Father, Son and Holy Spirit. Amen.
(from Eph. 3)

(A HYMN may be sung)

The Prayers

INTERCESSIONS
(Special thanksgivings and prayers …)
Father God,
by your grace we are your children:
through your Son we are redeemed from sin;
in the Spirit we are sent out as Christ's witnesses, and servants of your Kingdom.
We pray for the Church in its life and mission …
We pray for bishop N. and all ministers of the gospel …
We pray for new Christians, and those searching for you …
We pray for the suffering Church …
Make our lives bear witness to the gospel of Christ.
Lord, hear our prayer
and let our cry come to you.

We pray for the leaders of nations in the great responsibilities they bear …
We pray for our Queen and country …
We pray for the local community …
Make our lives to be of service to your Kingdom that is coming.
Lord, hear our prayer
and let our cry come to you.

We pray for people in need …
We pray for those who care for them …
Make us eager to help whoever needs us.
Lord, hear our prayer
and let our cry come to you.

We give thanks for all that is good in life.
Help us to appreciate each other's talents, and glorify God in the way we use them.
We remember with thanksgiving those who have died …
Grant us with them, and all the saints,
a share in your eternal Kingdom, through
Jesus Christ our Lord. Amen.

THE LORD'S PRAYER

(A HYMN may be sung)

CONCLUDING PRAYER
May the love of the Lord Jesus
draw us to himself,
the power of the Lord Jesus
strengthen us in his service, and
the joy of the Lord Jesus
fill our hearts. Amen.

(THE BLESSING may be said)

THE TWENTY-FIRST SUNDAY AFTER TRINITY
'Serving God with a quiet mind'

> In today's Collect we pray for 'pardon and peace'. Without these gifts we cannot fulfil all the possibilities that life offers us. A troubled conscience undermines any good we try to do. Today, may we find Christ's pardon and peace so that we can more fully serve God 'with a quiet mind'.

The Gathering

THE GREETING
Grace, mercy and peace from God our Father and the Lord Jesus Christ be with you. *(1 Tim. 1:2)*
And also with you.

(A HYMN may be sung)

Seek the Lord while he may be found,
call upon him while he is near.

Let the wicked forsake their way,
and the unrighteous their thoughts;

let them return to the Lord,
that he may have mercy upon them,

and to our God,
for he will abundantly pardon.
(Isa. 55:6-7)

PRAYER
Lord Jesus Christ,
give us the desire to seek first
God's will in all things.
Grant us the honesty to confess our sins,
and the humility to receive your forgiveness.
Help us to listen to your Word,
and show forth your love,
in lives of service and sacrifice. **Amen.**

(SONGS may be sung)

* * * * *

PENITENCE
Hear the words of comfort our Saviour Christ says to all who truly turn to him:
'Come to me, all who labour and are heavy laden, and I will give you rest.' *(Matt. 11:28)*

'God so loved the world that he gave his only Son, that whoever believes in him should not perish but have eternal life.' *(John 3:16)*

Hear what Saint Paul says: 'This saying is true and worthy of full acceptance, that Christ Jesus came into the world to save sinners.' *(1 Tim. 1:15)*

Let us confess our sins, in penitence and faith, firmly resolved to keep God's commandments and to live in love and peace with all.

***Almighty God, our heavenly Father,
we have sinned against you
and against our neighbour,
in thought and word and deed,
through negligence, through weakness,
through our own deliberate fault.
We are truly sorry,
and repent of all our sins.
For the sake of your Son Jesus Christ,
who died for us, forgive us all that is past; and grant that we may serve you
in newness of life,
to the glory of your name.*** **Amen.**

Almighty God,
who forgives all who truly repent,
have mercy upon *us*,
pardon and deliver *us* from all *our* sins,
confirm and strengthen *us* in all goodness,
and keep *us* in life eternal;
through Jesus Christ our Lord. **Amen.**

(The GLORIA, the VENITE, a SONG or RESPONSES may be used)

THE COLLECT OF THE DAY
Let us pray ... *(silent prayer)*

Grant, we beseech you, merciful Lord,
to your faithful people pardon and peace,
that they may be cleansed from all their sins
and serve you with a quiet mind;
through Jesus Christ your Son our Lord,
who is alive and reigns with you,
in the unity of the Holy Spirit,
one God, now and for ever. **Amen.**

The Liturgy of the Word

THE SCRIPTURE READING(S)

(After the reading)
This is the Word of the Lord.
Thanks be to God.

PSALM/HYMN or SCRIPTURAL SONG

THE GOSPEL
Hear the Gospel of our Lord Jesus Christ according to N.
Glory to you, O Lord.

(After the reading)
This is the Gospel of the Lord.
Praise to you, O Christ.

THE SERMON

AFFIRMATION OF FAITH
I believe in God, the Father almighty, creator of heaven and earth
I believe in Jesus Christ, his only Son, our Lord, who was conceived by the Holy Spirit, born of the Virgin Mary, suffered under Pontius Pilate, was crucified, died, and was buried; he descended to the dead.
On the third day he rose again; he ascended into heaven, he is seated at the right hand of the Father, and he will come to judge the living and the dead.
I believe in the Holy Spirit, the holy catholic Church, the communion of saints, the forgiveness of sins, the resurrection of the body, and the life everlasting. Amen.
(The Apostles' Creed)

(A HYMN may be sung)

The Prayers

INTERCESSIONS

(Special thanksgivings and prayers ...)

God our Father, we pray for your blessing on all people:

Bless our Queen and those who take authority in this and other nations ...
May they govern with wisdom and integrity, and bring justice and peace to the world:
Father of all, **in your mercy hear us.**

Bless those who lead the Church ...
May they be firm in faith, clear in vision, yet humble in your service:
Father of all, **in your mercy hear us.**

Bless those who teach, in schools, colleges and universities ...
May their skills help the young to achieve their best:
Father of all, **in your mercy hear us.**

Bless those who suffer from ill-health or pain, loneliness or loss ...
Deliver them from their distress and grant them healing, patience and peace:
Father of all, **in your mercy hear us.**

Bless those who care for the sick and frail ...
May they bring strength and encouragement to others, and know your grace for themselves:
Father of all, **in your mercy hear us.**

Bless those who go out to work each day ...
May they use their gifts for the common good, and bear witness to Christ in the service they render:
Father of all, **in your mercy hear us.**

We remember with thanksgiving those who have died ...
Father of all, **grant us with them, and all the saints, a share in your eternal Kingdom, through Christ our Lord. Amen.**

THE LORD'S PRAYER

(A HYMN may be sung)

CONCLUDING PRAYER
Lord, we pray that your grace may always precede and follow us, and make us continually to be given to all good works; through Jesus Christ our Lord. Amen.
(Collect from Common Worship)

(THE BLESSING may be said)

THE LAST SUNDAY AFTER TRINITY
(BIBLE SUNDAY)
'The Holy Scriptures: read, mark, learn and inwardly digest'

Today the long Trinity season in the Church year comes to an end. Its general theme has been the nourishing of Christian faith and discipleship. The image of spiritual 'nourishment' is highlighted today if it is also marked as **Bible Sunday**. The Collect asks God to help us read and 'inwardly digest' the Holy Scriptures so that we 'hold fast the hope of everlasting life ... in Jesus Christ'.

The Gathering

THE GREETING
The grace and mercy of our Lord Jesus Christ be with you.
And also with you.

(A HYMN may be sung)

Jesus said: 'One does not live by bread alone
but by every word that comes from the mouth of God.' *(Matt. 4:4)*

Lord, your Word is a lamp to my feet
and a light to my path. *(Ps. 119:105)*

PRAYER
*Heavenly Father,
in our time together now,
help us to celebrate your love,
learn from your truth,
trust in your grace,
and grow strong in your service,
through Jesus Christ our Lord.* **Amen.**

(SONGS may be sung)

* * * * *

PENITENCE
We are told in the Scriptures to measure our lives against the teaching of God's Word 'which is living and active, sharper than any two-edged sword ... it is able to judge the thoughts and intentions of the heart ...' *(Heb. 4:12-13)*

Let us therefore confess our failure to pattern our lives on the teaching of the Bible:

When we have neglected to read the Bible regularly and prayerfully.
Lord, have mercy.

When we have failed to listen to God's Word humbly and honestly.
Christ, have mercy.

When we have refused to apply its teaching to the way we live.
Lord, have mercy.

Hear what the Bible says: 'The saying is sure and worthy of full acceptance, that Christ Jesus came into the world to save sinners.' *(1 Tim. 1:15)*

May almighty God,
who sent his Son into the world to save sinners, bring *us* his pardon and peace,
now and for ever. **Amen.**

(The GLORIA, the VENITE, a SONG or RESPONSES may be used)

THE COLLECT OF THE DAY
Let us pray ... *(silent prayer)*

Blessed Lord,
who caused all Holy Scripture to be written for our learning: help us so to hear them,
to read, mark, learn and inwardly digest them that, through patience, and the comfort of your holy Word, we may embrace and for ever hold fast the hope of everlasting life, which you have given us in our Saviour Jesus Christ, who is alive and reigns with you, in the unity of the Holy Spirit,
one God, now and for ever. **Amen.**

The Liturgy of the Word

THE SCRIPTURE READING(S)

(After the reading)
This is the Word of the Lord.
Thanks be to God.

PSALM/HYMN or SCRIPTURAL SONG

THE GOSPEL
Hear the Gospel of our Lord Jesus Christ according to N.
Glory to you, O Lord.

(After the reading)
This is the Gospel of the Lord.
Praise to you, O Christ.

THE SERMON

AFFIRMATION OF FAITH
Let us declare our faith in the resurrection of our Lord Jesus Christ:

Christ died for our sins
in accordance with the Scriptures;
he was buried;
he was raised to life on the third day
in accordance with the Scriptures;
afterwards he appeared to his followers,
and to all the apostles:
this we have received,
and this we believe.   *(1 Cor. 15:3-7)*

This is the faith of the Church.
This is our faith.
We believe and trust in one God,
Father, Son and Holy Spirit.

(A HYMN may be sung)

The Prayers

INTERCESSIONS
(Special thanksgivings and prayers …)

Almighty God,
We give thanks that you reveal yourself to us when we engage with the text of the Bible. Give us the desire, and the discipline, to study its teaching, and to live what we learn.
Spirit of God,   **lead us into all truth.**

We give thanks for those who have translated the Bible into different languages. Bless the Bible Society in its work of making God's Word understandable and available to all.
Spirit of God,   **lead us into all truth.**

We give thanks for those who teach the Bible to young and old … Help them to show, with clarity and enthusiasm, the relevance of the Bible to life today.
Spirit of God,   **lead us into all truth.**

We give thanks for Bible discussion groups … May they bring fresh insights and encouragement to all who take part.
Spirit of God,   **lead us into all truth.**

We give thanks for theologians and teachers in colleges both here and overseas … Inspire them and their students in the teaching of God's Word.
Spirit of God,   **lead us into all truth.**

We give thanks for the health we have, and pray for those facing serious illness, painful treatment or failing health …
Spirit of God,
bring them healing, comfort and hope.

We remember with thanksgiving those who have died … Learning from their example, we pray for strength to follow him who is the incarnate Word, Jesus Christ our Lord.
           Amen.

THE LORD'S PRAYER

(A HYMN may be sung)

CONCLUDING PRAYER
Almighty God,
we thank you for the gift of your holy
word. May it be a lantern to our feet,
a light to our paths,
and a strength to our lives.
Take us and use us to love and to serve
in the power of the Holy Spirit
and in the name of your Son,
Jesus Christ our Lord.   *Amen.*
           (Collect from Common Worship)

(THE BLESSING or THE GRACE is said)

ALL SAINTS' SUNDAY
'Knit together in one communion and fellowship'

All Saints' Day, celebrated on or near 1 November, is an occasion of thanksgiving as we remember the faithful witness of countless Christians down the ages. We celebrate the lives of all who, in varied and in often testing circumstances, have shared in the Church's life and mission. According to St Paul, 'saints' (Latin *sanctus* – set apart for a special purpose) are what all Christians are called to be. (1 Cor. 1:2).

The Gathering

THE GREETING
Grace, mercy and peace to you from God.
May he fill us with truth and joy.

(A HYMN may be sung)

You are God and we praise you:
You are the Lord and we acclaim you.

The glorious company of apostles praise you.
The noble fellowship of prophets praise you.

The white-robed army of martyrs praise you.
Throughout the world the holy Church acclaims you:
Father of majesty unbounded;

Your true and only Son worthy of all worship, and the Holy Spirit advocate and guide.

Come then Lord and help your people, bought with the price of your own blood;
And bring us with your saints to glory everlasting.   *(from the Te Deum)*

PRAYER
Lord Jesus,
we thank you for your love
shown in the lives of all your saints:
those who lived in the past
and those living now;
those whose names are well known
and those whose names
are known only to you.   **Amen.**

(SONGS may be sung)

* * * * *

PENITENCE
The lives of the saints encourage us to persevere as Christ's followers, even when we stumble and falter: 'Since we are surrounded by so great a cloud of witnesses, let us lay aside every weight, and the sin that clings so closely, and let us run with perseverance the race that is set before us, looking to Jesus the pioneer and perfecter of our faith.'   *(Heb. 12:1)*

Let us confess our failings to Almighty God:

When we falter in faith or perseverance,
Lord, have mercy.

When we lack courage or commitment,
Christ, have mercy.

When we fail to show forgiveness or humility,
Lord, have mercy.

Almighty God,
who forgives all who truly repent,
have mercy upon *us,*
pardon and deliver *us* from all *our* sins,
confirm and strengthen *us* in all goodness,
and keep *us* in life eternal;
through Jesus Christ our Lord.   **Amen.**

(The GLORIA, the VENITE, a SONG or RESPONSES may be used)

THE COLLECT OF THE DAY
Let us pray …   *(silent prayer)*

Almighty God, you have knit together your elect in one communion and fellowship in the mystical body of your Son Christ our Lord: grant us grace so to follow your blessed saints in all virtuous and godly living that we may come to those inexpressible joys that you have prepared for those who truly love you; through Jesus Christ your Son our Lord, who is alive and reigns with you, in the unity of the Holy Spirit, one God, now and for ever.   **Amen.**

The Liturgy of the Word

THE SCRIPTURE READING(S)

(After the reading)
This is the Word of the Lord.
Thanks be to God.

PSALM/HYMN or SCRIPTURAL SONG

THE GOSPEL

Hear the Gospel of our Lord Jesus Christ according to N.
Glory to you, O Lord.

(After the reading)
This is the Gospel of the Lord.
Praise to you, O Christ.

THE SERMON

AFFIRMATION OF FAITH

I believe in God, the Father almighty, creator of heaven and earth

I believe in Jesus Christ, his only Son, our Lord, who was conceived by the Holy Spirit, born of the Virgin Mary, suffered under Pontius Pilate, was crucified, died, and was buried; he descended to the dead. On the third day he rose again; he ascended into heaven, he is seated at the right hand of the Father, and he will come to judge the living and the dead. I believe in the Holy Spirit, the holy catholic Church, the communion of saints, the forgiveness of sins, the resurrection of the body, and the life everlasting. **Amen.**
(The Apostles' Creed)

(A HYMN may be sung)

(Candles may be lit in honour of particular people whose memory is personally treasured).

The Prayers

INTERCESSIONS

(Special thanksgivings and prayers ...)

Father in heaven: we give thanks for the communion of saints. May their witness inspire us, and their fellowship sustain us.
Come Lord, **and help your people.**

We give thanks for the faith of the apostles, the vision of prophets, the boldness of evangelists, and the compassion of social reformers, whose lives shine from the Bible and Church history ... Teach us, through their stories, what it means to follow Christ.
Come Lord, **and help your people.**

We give thanks for all who have quietly borne witness to Christ through the quality of their lives and the depth of their love ...
Give us a heart that cares about others, at home, at work, in the neighbourhood, and in all situations of struggle or need.
Come Lord, **and help your people.**

We give thanks for the courage of martyrs and all who suffer for their beliefs ...
Strengthen us to stand firm for Christ in the face of mockery or persecution.
Come Lord, **and help your people.**

We give thanks for those who have been our guide at different stages of our faith journey ... Help us support each other as we move forward on our earthly pilgrimage.
Come Lord, **and help your people.**

We give thanks for those who have died, leaving us with inspiring memories ...
Fulfil our hope of eternal life in Christ.
Come Lord and help your people, bought with the price of your own blood, and bring us with your saints to glory everlasting. Amen.
(from the Te Deum)

THE LORD'S PRAYER

(A HYMN may be sung)

CONCLUDING PRAYER

With all the saints in heaven and on earth we join our prayers and praises:
**Blessing and glory and wisdom
And thanksgiving and honour and power
Be to our God forever and ever. Amen.**
(Rev. 7:12)

(THE BLESSING or THE GRACE is said)

THE FOURTH SUNDAY BEFORE ADVENT
'The flame of love'

In every human heart there is the flicker of love, implanted by the God of love. For the saints, God has – in the words of today's Collect – kindled that flicker into 'the flame of love', generating in them an intense faith and a powerful love. During this All Saints-tide, 'we rejoice in the triumphs of the saints and are sustained by their example and fellowship'.

The Gathering

THE GREETING
Praise our God, all you his servants
and all who fear him, small and great.
(Rev. 19:5)

(A HYMN may be sung)

Happy are those whose way is blameless,
who walk in the law of the Lord.

Happy are those who keep his decrees,
who seek him with their whole heart,

who also do not wrong,
but walk in his ways. *(Ps. 119:1-3)*

PRAYER
God, our Father in heaven,
we thank you for your grace,
which has changed ordinary people
into saints, and servants of your
Kingdom.
Help us, like them, to reflect your light
and to bear witness to your love
through Jesus Christ our Lord. **Amen.**

(SONGS may be sung)

* * * * *

PENITENCE
The lives of the saints encourage us to persevere as Christ's followers, even when we stumble and falter: 'Since we are surrounded by so great a cloud of witnesses, let us lay aside every weight, and the sin that clings so closely, and let us run with perseverance the race that is set before us, looking to Jesus the pioneer and perfecter of our faith.' *(Heb. 12:1)*

Let us confess our sins and failings to Almighty God:

Almighty God, our heavenly Father,
we have sinned against you
and against our neighbour,
in thought and word and deed,
through negligence, through weakness,
through our own deliberate fault.
We are truly sorry
and repent of all our sins.
For the sake of your Son Jesus Christ,
who died for us,
forgive us all that is past;
and grant that we may serve you
in newness of life
to the glory of your name. **Amen.**

May almighty God have mercy on *us*,
forgive *us* our sins,
and bring *us* to everlasting life,
through Jesus Christ our Lord. **Amen.**

(The GLORIA, the VENITE, a SONG or RESPONSES may be used)

THE COLLECT OF THE DAY
Let us pray … *(silent prayer)*

Almighty and eternal God,
you have kindled the flame of love in the hearts of the saints:
grant to us the same faith and power of love,
that, as we rejoice in their triumphs,
we may be sustained by their example and fellowship;
through Jesus Christ your Son our Lord,
who is alive and reigns with you,
in the unity of the Holy Spirit,
one God, now and for ever. **Amen.**

The Liturgy of the Word

THE SCRIPTURE READING(S)

(After the reading)
This is the Word of the Lord.
Thanks be to God.

PSALM/HYMN or SCRIPTURAL SONG

THE GOSPEL

Hear the Gospel of our Lord Jesus Christ according to N.
Glory to you, O Lord.

(After the reading)
This is the Gospel of the Lord.
Praise to you, O Christ.

THE SERMON

AFFIRMATION OF FAITH

We affirm our faith in God:
**I believe in God, the Father almighty, creator of heaven and earth.
I believe in Jesus Christ, his only Son, our Lord, who was conceived by the Holy Spirit, born of the Virgin Mary, suffered under Pontius Pilate, was crucified, died, and was buried; he descended to the dead. On the third day he rose again; he ascended into heaven, he is seated at the right hand of the Father, and he will come to judge the living and the dead.
I believe in the Holy Spirit, the holy catholic Church, the communion of saints, the forgiveness of sins, the resurrection of the body, and the life everlasting. Amen.**
(The Apostles' Creed)

(A HYMN may be sung)

The Prayers

INTERCESSIONS

(Special thanksgivings and prayers ...)

Our Father in heaven, we give thanks for the church and for all that we receive through its worship, teaching and fellowship. We pray for bishop N. and the life of this diocese ... For each other here and all who minister among us ... For our fellow Christians in other places ... Renew us by the Holy Spirit that we may grow as disciples of Christ.
Lord God, **hear our prayer.**

We give thanks for this nation and those in authority who serve the people with integrity and dedication. We pray:
for our Queen and government ... For all who shape our culture, especially those working in the media ... For people anywhere suffering from disaster, war or oppression ... Bring justice to all, and the opportunity to make the most of their lives.
Lord God, **hear our prayer.**

We give thanks for our community, and for those who cherish us. Strengthen the bonds of trust between husbands and wives, parents and children, friends and neighbours.
Lord God, **hear our prayer.**

We give thanks for the health we have, and for the skills of those who attend to us when we are in need. Bring healing and encouragement to those suffering from ill-health, depression or frailty ...
Lord God, **hear our prayer.**

We give thanks for those whose memory we treasure ...
Grant us with them, and with all the saints ... the joy of eternal life
in Christ our Lord. **Amen.**

THE LORD'S PRAYER

(A HYMN may be sung)

CONCLUDING PRAYER

***May the grace of Christ our Saviour,
and the Father's boundless love,
with the Holy Spirit's favour,
rest upon us from above.***

***Thus may we abide in union
with each other and the Lord,
and possess, in sweet communion,
joys which earth cannot afford. Amen.***
(J. Newton)

(The BLESSING may be said)

THE THIRD SUNDAY BEFORE ADVENT
'Govern the hearts and minds of those in authority'

If Jesus Christ is 'the King of all' – as today's Collect says – earthly rulers take their authority from him and are entrusted with the task of extending 'his just and gentle rule', in a world that is 'divided and torn apart by the ravages of sin'. We remember all leaders today and pray that governments will themselves be 'governed' by Christ as they serve the people.

The Gathering

THE GREETING
Grace, mercy and peace from God
our Father and the Lord Jesus Christ
be with you.
And also with you. *(1 Tim. 1:2)*

(A HYMN may be sung)

Bless the Lord, O my soul,
and all that is within me, bless his holy name.
The Lord has established his throne in the heavens,
and his Kingdom rules over all.
Bless the Lord, all his hosts,
his ministers that do his will.
Bless the Lord, all his works, in all places of his dominion.
Bless the Lord, O my soul.
(Ps. 103:1, 19, 21-22)

PRAYER
Lord Jesus Christ, our Servant King,
guide all leaders to use their authority,
not as a way of promoting
their own interests, not as a way of having
power over other people, but as an
opportunity to serve them. **Amen.**

(SONGS may be sung)

* * * * *

PENITENCE
We bring to God our sins, and the sins of humanity, that spread hatred and distrust in the world:

When leaders are corrupted and freedom is crushed:
Lord, have mercy. **Lord, have mercy.**

When minorities are blamed and the weak are exploited:
Christ, have mercy. **Christ, have mercy.**

When nations go to war and peace-makers are ignored:
Lord, have mercy. **Lord, have mercy.**

Let us confess our sins, in penitence and faith, firmly resolved to keep God's commandments and to live in love and peace with all.
**Most merciful God,
Father of our Lord Jesus Christ,
we confess that we have sinned
in thought, word and deed.
We have not loved you with our whole heart. We have not loved our neighbours as ourselves.
In your mercy forgive what we have been,
help us to amend what we are,
and direct what we shall be;
that we may do justly, love mercy,
and walk humbly with you, our God.
Amen.**

May almighty God have mercy on *us*,
forgive *us* our sins,
and bring *us* to everlasting life,
through Jesus Christ our Lord. **Amen.**

(The GLORIA, the VENITE, a SONG or RESPONSES may be used)

THE COLLECT OF THE DAY
Let us pray ... *(silent prayer)*

Almighty Father, whose will is to restore all things in your beloved Son, the King of all: govern the hearts and minds of those in authority, and bring the families of the nations, divided and torn apart by the ravages of sin, to be subject to his just and gentle rule; who is alive and reigns with you, in the unity of the Holy Spirit, one God, now and for ever. **Amen.**

The Liturgy of the Word

THE SCRIPTURE READING(S)

(After the reading)
This is the Word of the Lord.
Thanks be to God.

PSALM/HYMN or SCRIPTURAL SONG

THE GOSPEL
Hear the Gospel of our Lord Jesus Christ according to N.
Glory to you, O Lord.

(After the reading)
This is the Gospel of the Lord.
Praise to you, O Christ.

THE SERMON

AFFIRMATION OF FAITH
We declare our faith in God:

Do you believe and trust in God the Father, source of all being and life, the one for whom we exist?
We believe and trust in him.

Do you believe and trust in God the Son who took our human nature, died for us, and rose again?
We believe and trust in him.

Do you believe and trust in God the Holy Spirit, who gives life to the people of God and makes Christ known in the world?
We believe and trust in him.

This is the faith of the Church.
This is our faith.
We believe and trust in one God, Father, Son and Holy Spirit.

(A HYMN may be sung)

The Prayers

INTERCESSIONS
(Special thanksgivings and prayers …)
Lord God, we pray for all who lead:

We pray for our Queen, the Prime Minister, Cabinet Ministers, Members of Parliament and all who make important decisions in the nation's life … Guide those who lead us that we may be well and wisely governed.
Your Kingdom come, **your will be done.**

We pray for other nations, especially where there is bitter conflict or ethnic tension … Give courage to all who work for peace and justice in this divided world, and bless the work of the United Nations.
Your Kingdom come, **your will be done.**

We pray for church leaders and all who are called to minister among us …
Grant them the gifts of the Holy Spirit for the upbuilding of Christ's people in faith and understanding, fellowship and mission.
Your Kingdom come, **your will be done.**

We pray for the managers of businesses and organizations …
May the creative skills of hands and brains be harnessed for the good of all.
Your Kingdom come, **your will be done.**

We pray for the heads of schools and all places of education … Help teachers bring the best out of their students.
Your Kingdom come, **your will be done.**

We pray for parents as they seek to build strong family life … Give them love and perseverance as they guide their children to adulthood.
Your Kingdom come, **your will be done.**

We remember with thanksgiving those who have died … Entrusting them to your mercy, we offer ourselves in the service of your Kingdom, through Christ our Lord. **Amen.**

THE LORD'S PRAYER

(A HYMN may be sung)

CONCLUDING PRAYER
Lead us from death to life, from falsehood to truth. Lead us from despair to hope, from fear to trust. Lead us from hate to love, from war to peace.
Let peace fill our hearts, our world, our universe, for Jesus' sake. **Amen.**
(International Prayer for Peace)

(THE BLESSING or THE GRACE is said)

THE SECOND SUNDAY BEFORE ADVENT
'Be made like Jesus in his glorious Kingdom'

As we draw near to the end of the Church Year, and look forward to Advent and the start of a new one, we are reminded in today's Collect of the ultimate purpose of our lives: to become 'like Jesus Christ – in his glorious Kingdom'. This is only possible because Christ has 'destroyed the works of the devil and made us the children of God and heirs of eternal life'.

The Gathering

THE GREETING
Grace, mercy and peace from God
our Father and the Lord Jesus Christ
be with you.
And also with you. *(1 Tim. 1:2)*

(A HYMN may be sung)

See what love the Father has given us, that
we should be called children of God;
and that is what we are.

Beloved, we are God's children now:
what we will be has not yet been revealed.

What we do know is this:
when Christ is revealed, we will be like him,
for we will see him as he is.

And all who have this hope in him purify themselves,
just as he is pure. *(1 John 3:1-3)*

PRAYER
O Lord,
open our eyes to see what is beautiful,
our minds to know what is true,
and our hearts to seek what is good,
for Jesus' sake. **Amen.**

(SONGS may be sung)

* * * * *

PENITENCE
As we bow humbly before God we remember how our lives are often marred by impurity and insincerity …

Let us confess our sins in penitence and faith:

When we try to present a good image rather than to purify our hearts …
Lord, have mercy. **Lord, have mercy.**

When we seek to please others rather than to speak the truth …
Christ, have mercy. **Christ, have mercy.**

When we are slow to admit that others may be right, or to say sorry if we are in the wrong …
Lord, have mercy. **Lord, have mercy.**

When we honour God with our lips but keep him far from our hearts …
Christ, have mercy. **Christ, have mercy.**

May almighty God have mercy on *us*,
forgive *us our* sins,
and bring *us* to everlasting life,
through Jesus Christ our Lord. **Amen.**

(The GLORIA, the VENITE, a SONG or RESPONSES may be used)

THE COLLECT OF THE DAY
Let us pray … *(silent prayer)*

Heavenly Father, whose blessed Son was revealed to destroy the works of the devil and to make us the children of God and heirs of eternal life: grant that we, having this hope, may purify ourselves even as he is pure; that when he shall appear in power and great glory we may be made like him in his eternal and glorious Kingdom;
where he is alive and reigns with you,
in the unity of the Holy Spirit, one God,
now and for ever. **Amen.**

The Liturgy of the Word

THE SCRIPTURE READING(S)

(After the reading)
This is the Word of the Lord.
Thanks be to God.

PSALM/HYMN or SCRIPTURAL SONG

THE GOSPEL
Hear the Gospel of our Lord Jesus Christ according to N.
Glory to you, O Lord.

(After the reading)
This is the Gospel of the Lord.
Praise to you, O Christ.

THE SERMON

AFFIRMATION OF FAITH
Let us declare our faith in God:

We believe in God the Father,
from whom every family
in heaven and on earth is named.

We believe in God the Son,
who lives in our hearts through faith,
and fills us with his love.

We believe in God the Holy Spirit,
who strengthens us
with power from on high.

We believe in one God;
Father, Son and Holy Spirit.   Amen.
(from Eph. 3).

(A HYMN may be sung)

The Prayers

INTERCESSIONS
(Special thanksgivings and prayers ...)

We bring to you, Father God, the needs of all people, for whose salvation you sent your Son Jesus Christ:

We pray for our Queen and government, and the leaders of the nations ... We think of people divided by national enmity, religious intolerance, or racial prejudice ...
Lord Jesus, where there is hatred,
let me sow love.

We pray for husbands and wives, parents and children, employers and employees ... We think of families, communities and work places where relationships have broken down ...
Lord Jesus, where there is injury,
let me sow pardon.

We pray for bishop N., for all who teach the Christian faith, and for the life of our church. We think of those whose faith is being sorely tested ...
Lord Jesus, where there is doubt,
let me sow faith.

We remember with thanksgiving those who have died ... We think of all who are overshadowed by loss or loneliness ... We pray for all in need ... We pray for their families and friends, doctors, nurses and carers.
Lord Jesus, where there is despair,
let me give hope.

We think of ourselves, our self-centredness, our faltering attempts to serve you ...
Lord Jesus,
**make us channels of your peace
and witnesses of your Kingdom.**   Amen.

THE LORD'S PRAYER

(A HYMN may be sung)

CONCLUDING PRAYER
**Lead us from death to life, from falsehood to truth. Lead us from despair to hope, from fear to trust. Lead us from hate to love, from war to peace.
Let peace fill our hearts, our world, our universe, for Jesus' sake.**   Amen.
(International Prayer for Peace)

(THE BLESSING or THE GRACE is said)

'CHRIST THE KING'
THE SUNDAY NEXT BEFORE ADVENT

The Church Year ends today, with the celebration of 'Christ the King'. The Collect expresses the hope that God, having crowned his Son on Ascension Day as the 'ruler over all things', will one day 'bring the whole created order to worship at his feet'. Next Sunday (Advent) we begin a new Church Year, praying for that day when he will come again and be acclaimed as King.

The Gathering

THE GREETING
The grace and mercy of our Lord Jesus Christ be with you.
And also with you.

(A HYMN may be sung)

Great and amazing are your deeds, Lord God the Almighty!
Just and true are your ways, King of the nations!

Lord, who will not fear and glorify your name?
For you alone are holy.

All nations will come and worship before you,
for your judgements have been revealed.
(Rev. 15:3-4)

PRAYER
God our Father, we give thanks
that you raised your Son from death to life,
and exalted him to your throne in glory.
Send the Holy Spirit
that we may worship him as our Lord,
and serve him as our King,
for Jesus Christ's sake. **Amen.**

(SONGS may be sung)

* * * * *

PENITENCE
As we anticipate the rule of Christ over all things, we recognize the evil which still disfigures God's world, and accept our shared human responsibility for it …

Lord Jesus Christ, we confess:

The widening gap between the comfortably-off and the desperately poor …
Lord, have mercy. **Lord, have mercy.**

The deep divisions between nations, races and religions …
Christ, have mercy. **Christ, have mercy.**

The weakening of family life and the decay of communities …
Lord, have mercy. **Lord, have mercy.**

The damage inflicted upon the earth through insatiable consumer greed …
Christ, have mercy. **Christ, have mercy.**

The loss of faith, and erosion of Christian values …
Lord, have mercy. **Lord, have mercy.**

May God who loved the world so much
that he sent his Son to be our Saviour,
forgive *us our* sins
and make us holy to serve him in the world,
through Jesus Christ our Lord. **Amen.**

(The GLORIA, the VENITE, a SONG or RESPONSES may be used)

THE COLLECT OF THE DAY
Let us pray … *(silent prayer)*

Eternal Father, whose Son Jesus Christ
ascended to the throne of heaven that he
might rule over all things as Lord and King:
keep the Church in the unity of the Spirit and
in the bond of peace, and bring the whole
created order to worship at his feet;
who is alive and reigns with you,
in the unity of the Holy Spirit,
one God, now and for ever. **Amen.**

The Liturgy of the Word

THE SCRIPTURE READING(S)

(After the reading)
This is the Word of the Lord.
Thanks be to God.

PSALM/HYMN or SCRIPTURAL SONG

THE GOSPEL

Hear the Gospel of our Lord Jesus Christ according to N.
Glory to you, O Lord.

(After the reading)
This is the Gospel of the Lord.
Praise to you, O Christ.

THE SERMON

AFFIRMATION OF FAITH

Let us affirm our faith in Jesus Christ the Son of God:

Though he was divine,
he did not cling to equality with God,
but made himself nothing.
Taking the form of a slave,
he was born in human likeness.
He humbled himself, and was obedient
to death – even the death of the cross.
Therefore God has raised him on high,
and given him the name above every
name: that at the name of Jesus
every knee should bow,
and every voice proclaim
that Jesus Christ is Lord,
to the glory of God the Father
(Phil. 2:6-11)

This is the faith of the Church.
This is our faith.
We believe and trust in one God,
Father, Son and Holy Spirit. **Amen.**

(A HYMN may be sung)

The Prayers

INTERCESSIONS

(Special thanksgivings and prayers …)

Father in heaven, we give thanks that your Son was raised from the humiliation of the cross to the glory of heaven. We offer our prayers through him who, as our great High Priest, ever intercedes for us.

We pray for all who serve his Church as bishops *(N.)* priests, deacons and lay ministers … Give them grace to nourish your people through spiritual worship, sound teaching and pastoral care.
Your Kingdom come. **Your will be done.**

We pray for our Christian brothers and sisters in other places who are persecuted, hated or deprived … Sustain their faith, and strengthen our fellowship with them through prayer and practical support.
Your Kingdom come. **Your will be done.**

We pray for each other as we seek to be witnesses of Christ in our everyday lives and work … Lead us by the Holy Spirit in the ways of Christ, that we may learn to speak and do as he would.
Your Kingdom come. **Your will be done.**

We pray for our Queen and government, and for the leaders of the nations, as they try to resolve the difficult issues confronting them … Make them know they are accountable to God and guide them into policies that promote justice, reconciliation and opportunity for all.
Your Kingdom come. **Your will be done.**

We pray for those who face distressing illness, increasing frailty or painful treatment … Bring healing through the care they receive from doctors and nurses, relatives and friends.
Your Kingdom come. **Your will be done.**

We remember those who have died …
Father raise us, with all who have died in faith, to eternal life in Christ. **Amen.**

THE LORD'S PRAYER

(A HYMN may be sung)

CONCLUDING PRAYER

Jesus, Saviour and King, we have
honoured you with our lips, help us also
to offer you our lives that through us your
light may shine. **Amen.**

(THE BLESSING or THE GRACE is said)

THE TRANSFIGURATION OF OUR LORD
'Give us strength to hear his voice'

Today we recall a turning point in Jesus' life. In a startling disclosure on the mountain, the disciples were shown that he was not only the one who fulfilled the old religion of Israel (represented by Moses and Elijah) but also the beloved Son of God who would forge a 'way out' (Greek *exodus*) of the old, into a new, living relationship with God.

The Gathering

THE GREETING
The Lord of glory be with you.
The Lord bless you.

(A HYMN may be sung)

The Lord is King.
Let the peoples tremble!

He sits enthroned upon the cherubim.
Let the earth quake!

Let them praise your great and awesome Name.
Holy is he!

Moses and Aaron were among his priests:
They cried to the Lord and he answered them.

Extol the Lord our God, and worship at his holy mountain.
For the Lord our God is holy.
(Ps. 99:1-3, 6, 9)

PRAYER
Almighty God,
to whom all hearts are open,
all desires known, and from whom no secrets are hidden:
cleanse the thoughts of our hearts
by the inspiration of your Holy Spirit,
that we may perfectly love you,
and worthily magnify your holy name;
through Christ our Lord. **Amen.**

(SONGS may be sung)

* * * * *

PENITENCE
A cloud overshadowed them, and from the cloud there came a voice, 'This is my Son, the Beloved; listen to him!' *(Mark 9:7)*

Father, we confess that we have not paid heed to the teaching of your Son Jesus Christ. Too often we have followed our own selfish desires and neglected the needs of others. *(silence)*

Let us confess our sins in penitence and faith.
Almighty God, our heavenly Father,
we have sinned against you
and against our neighbour
in thought and word and deed,
through negligence, through weakness,
through our own deliberate fault.
We are truly sorry
and repent of all our sins.
For the sake of your Son Jesus Christ,
who died for us,
forgive us all that is past and grant that
we may serve you in newness of life;
to the glory of your name. **Amen.**

May Almighty God have mercy on *us*,
forgive *us our* sins,
and bring *us* to everlasting life,
through Jesus Christ our Lord. **Amen.**

(The GLORIA, the VENITE, a SONG or RESPONSES may be used)

THE COLLECT OF THE DAY
Let us pray ... *(silent prayer)*

Father in heaven, whose Son Jesus Christ was wonderfully transfigured before chosen witnesses upon the holy mountain, and spoke of the exodus he would accomplish at Jerusalem: grant us strength so to hear his voice and bear our cross that in the world to come we may see him as he is; who is alive and reigns with you, in the unity of the Holy Spirit, one God, now and for ever. **Amen.**

The Liturgy of the Word

THE SCRIPTURE READING(S)

(After the reading)
This is the Word of the Lord.
Thanks be to God.

PSALM/HYMN or SCRIPTURAL SONG

THE GOSPEL
Hear the Gospel of our Lord Jesus Christ according to N.
Glory to you, O Lord.

(After the reading)
This is the Gospel of the Lord.
Praise to you, O Christ.

THE SERMON

AFFIRMATION OF FAITH
I believe in God, the Father almighty, creator of heaven and earth.
I believe in Jesus Christ, his only Son, our Lord,
who was conceived by the Holy Spirit, born of the Virgin Mary,
suffered under Pontius Pilate, was crucified, died and was buried; he descended to the dead.
On the third day he rose again; he ascended into heaven,
he is seated at the right hand of the Father
and he will come to judge the living and the dead.
I believe in the Holy Spirit, the holy catholic Church, the communion of saints, the forgiveness of sins, the resurrection of the body, and the life everlasting. **Amen.**
(The Apostles' Creed)

(A HYMN may be sung)

The Prayers

INTERCESSIONS
(Special thanksgivings and prayers ...)

Our Father in heaven, we bring to you the needs of the world, knowing that you hear our prayers and work out your good purposes through those who believe.

We pray for the Church in this diocese: for our bishops, clergy and lay ministers...
Send more people to serve Christ in his Church, here and overseas, both lay and ordained, part-time and full-time...
Bless all who are in training for ministry...
Grant us your Holy Spirit that together we may walk in the way of Christ.
Lord of glory, **shine upon us.**

We pray for our Queen and country, and for all nations and their leaders... strengthen them, and us, to work for justice, search for peace and overcome evil with good.
Lord of glory, **shine upon us.**

We pray for families to be loving and stable, and our community to be caring and vibrant... Help those in difficulty to find the right way through their problems.
Lord of glory, **shine upon us.**

We pray for those suffering pain or ill-health ... for the mentally or emotionally distressed ... Bring strength, healing and encouragement through those who care ...
Lord of glory, **shine upon us.**

We give thanks for those who have died ... Grant us with them the joy of eternal life in Christ.
Lord of glory, **shine upon us.**

Father, we remember your many blessings, given to us each day. We ask for grace to become more like your Son, Jesus Christ our Lord. **Amen.**

THE LORD'S PRAYER

(A HYMN may be sung)

CONCLUDING PRAYER
Grant, Lord, that we may hold to you without parting, worship without wearying, serve you without failing; faithfully seek you, happily find you, and for ever possess you, the only God, blessed now and always. **Amen.**
(St Anselm)

(THE BLESSING or THE GRACE is said)

HARVEST FESTIVAL
'God gives us the fruits of the earth'

Harvest Festival has its origins in the Jewish Feast of the Ingathering. It is a thanksgiving for **God's care** towards his people, for his **gifts** that produce the harvest (sun and rain, soil and seeds, plants and animals) and for his **partners** in the harvest: farmers, fishermen and producers. We remember also the **Industrial Harvest** that turns the earth's minerals into energy and implements for human use.

The Gathering

THE GREETING
The grace and mercy of our Lord Jesus Christ be with you.
And also with you.

(A HYMN may be sung)

Thank you, God, for the harvest,
and for all the work that people do:

For farmers near and far,
ploughing and sowing,
tending and reaping the crops,
caring for flocks and herds,
God, we give you thanks
and bless your holy name.

For fishermen and sea-farers,
who bring us food from far-off places,
God, we give you thanks
and bless your holy name.

For bakers and producers, drivers and traders who fill the shops with food,
God we give you thanks
and bless your holy name.

For miners and oil rig workers
who toil in danger, supplying energy for factories, and warmth for our homes,
God, we give you thanks
and bless your holy name.

For workers in industry and commerce
who use technology to provide us with goods and services,
God, we give you thanks
and bless your holy name.

For your gifts of soil and seeds, sunshine and rain, and the miracle of nature's life,
God, we give you thanks
and bless your holy name.

OFFERING OF HARVEST GIFTS
(The gifts are brought up. At the end, a member of the congregation says to the minister:)
**We bring these gifts to God
in thankfulness for the harvest:
He has given us everything we need.**

God, our Father in heaven,
who created us and sustains our life,
accept these harvest gifts as a sign of our appreciation for your unfailing love.
May they bring blessing to the people who receive them;
through Jesus Christ our Lord. **Amen.**

Yours, Lord, is the greatness, the power, the glory, the splendour, and the majesty. for everything in heaven and on earth is yours. All things come from you, and of your own do we give you.

(SONGS may be sung)

* * * * *

PENITENCE
Let us confess our sins against God, and mankind's abuse of his Creation:

When we demand cheap food without thought of the well-being of the growers, the farm animals or the land itself ...
Lord, have mercy. **Lord, have mercy.**

When we fail to consider those who produce our food in difficult conditions for meagre rewards ...
Christ, have mercy. **Christ, have mercy.**

When we forget to give thanks to God for good food and clean water ...
Lord, have mercy. **Lord, have mercy.**

May almighty God have mercy on *us*,
forgive *us our* sins
and bring *us* to everlasting life,
through Jesus Christ our Lord. **Amen.**

THE COLLECT OF THE DAY
Let us pray …   *(silent prayer)*

Eternal God, you crown the year with your goodness and you give us the fruits of the earth in their season:
grant that we may use them to your glory,
for the relief of those in need
and for our own well-being,
through Jesus Christ your Son our Lord,
who is alive and reigns with you,
in the unity of the Holy Spirit,
one God, now and for ever.   **Amen.**

The Liturgy of the Word

THE SCRIPTURE READING(S)
(After the reading)
This is the Word of the Lord.
Thanks be to God.

PSALM or HYMN

THE GOSPEL
Hear the Gospel of our Lord Jesus Christ according to N.
Glory to you, O Lord.
(After the reading)
This is the Gospel of the Lord.
Praise to you, O Christ.

THE SERMON

AFFIRMATION OF FAITH
Let us affirm our faith in God:

Do you believe and trust in God the Father,
source of all being and life, the one for whom we exist?
We believe and trust in him.

Do you believe and trust in God the Son,
who took our human nature,
died for us and rose again?
We believe and trust in him.

Do you believe and trust in God the Holy Spirit, who gives life to the people of God
and makes Christ known in the world?
We believe and trust in him.

This is the faith of the Church.
***This is our faith.
We believe and trust in one God,
Father, Son and Holy Spirit.***   **Amen.**

(A HYMN may be sung)

The Prayers

INTERCESSIONS
(Special thanksgivings and prayers …)
Lord God, you promised to Noah that while the earth remains, seed-time and harvest, cold and heat, summer and winter, day and night shall not cease.
We offer now our harvest prayers:

Lord of the Harvest, who gives us our daily bread, we pray for all who work on farms, in industry, and on the high seas. We ask for your blessing on their work so that all may enjoy the fruit of their labour.
Lord of the Harvest,   ***hear our prayer.***

Loving Lord, who has given us such a diverse and beautiful world to live in, give us respect for animals; help us to prosper without polluting the earth with waste and toxic chemicals; teach us to be gentle with this good earth, on which our life depends
Lord of the Harvest,   ***hear our prayer.***

God our Creator, make us more thankful for what we have received, more content with what we have, and more generous to others.
Lord of the Harvest,   ***hear our prayer.***

Father God, we pray for all who suffer from drought and disasters, war and oppression, disease and pain …
Strengthen them with hope and perseverance, and bless all who go to their help,
through Jesus Christ our Lord.   **Amen.**

THE LORD'S PRAYER
(A HYMN may be sung)

CONCLUDING PRAYER
May the road rise to meet you;
may the wind be always at your back,
may the rain fall softly upon your fields;
may God hold you in the hollow of his hand.
Amen.   *(Gaelic blessing)*

(THE BLESSING or THE GRACE is said)

A SAINT'S DAY
'Bring us with your saints to glory'

Some of the marks of a saint (Latin *sanctus* – set apart for a special purpose) are: **openness** to the Spirit of God and the insight he gives; **dependence** on the grace of Christ for forgiveness and strength; and **commitment** to serving Christ in whatever way he calls. Today we remember one saint whose witness (Greek *martus*) challenges, inspires and encourages us.

The Gathering

THE GREETING

Grace, mercy and peace to you from God.
May he fill us with truth and joy.

(A HYMN may be sung)

You are God and we praise you:
You are the Lord and we acclaim you.

The glorious company of apostles praise you.
The noble fellowship of prophets praise you.

The white-robed army of martyrs praise you.
Throughout the world the holy Church acclaims you:
Father of majesty unbounded;

Your true and only Son worthy of all worship.
And the Holy Spirit advocate and guide.

Come then Lord and help your people,
bought with the price of your own blood;
and bring us with your saints
to glory everlasting. *(from the Te Deum)*

PRAYER

Almighty Father,
you have built up your Church
through the love and devotion of your saints:
inspire us to follow the example of N.
whom we commemorate today,
that we in our generation may rejoice with
him/her in the vision of your glory;
through Jesus Christ your Son our Lord,
who is alive and reigns with you,
in the unity of the Holy Spirit,
one God, now and for ever. **Amen.**
(Collect from Common Worship)

(SONGS may be sung)
* * * * *

PENITENCE

The lives of the saints encourage us to persevere as Christ's followers: 'Since we are surrounded by so great a cloud of witnesses, let us lay aside every weight, and the sin that clings so closely, and let us run with perseverance the race that is set before us, looking to Jesus the pioneer and perfecter of our faith.' *(Heb. 12:1)*

When we falter in faith or perseverance,
Lord, have mercy.

When we lack courage or commitment,
Christ, have mercy.

When we fail to show forgiveness or humility,
Lord, have mercy.

Let us confess our sins to God:

Almighty God, our heavenly Father,
we have sinned against you and against
our neighbour in thought and word and
deed, through negligence, through
weakness, through our own deliberate
fault. We are truly sorry and repent of all
our sins For the sake of your Son Jesus
Christ, who died for us, forgive us all that
is past and grant that we may serve you
in newness of life to the glory of your
name. **Amen.**

May almighty God have mercy on *us*,
forgive *us our* sins,
and bring *us* to everlasting life,
through Jesus Christ our Lord. **Amen.**

(THE GLORIA, the VENITE, a SONG or RESPONSES may be used)

THE COLLECT OF THE DAY

Let us pray ... *(silent prayer)*

The Liturgy of the Word

THE SCRIPTURE READING(S)

(After the reading)
This is the Word of the Lord.
Thanks be to God.

PSALM/HYMN or SCRIPTURAL SONG

THE GOSPEL

Hear the Gospel of our Lord Jesus Christ according to N.
Glory to you, O Lord.

(After the reading)
This is the Gospel of the Lord.
Praise to you, O Christ.

THE SERMON

AFFIRMATION OF FAITH

I believe in God, the Father almighty, creator of heaven and earth.
I believe in Jesus Christ, his only Son, our Lord, who was conceived by the Holy Spirit, born of the Virgin Mary, suffered under Pontius Pilate, was crucified, died, and was buried; he descended to the dead. On the third day he rose again; he ascended into heaven, he is seated at the right hand of the Father, and he will come to judge the living and the dead.
I believe in the Holy Spirit, the holy catholic Church, the communion of saints, the forgiveness of sins, the resurrection of the body, and the life everlasting. **Amen.**

(The Apostles' Creed)

(A HYMN may be sung)

The Prayers

INTERCESSIONS

(Special thanksgivings and prayers …)

We pray, Father in heaven:

For all Christian people, knit together by their faith in Jesus; for bishop N. and for all who teach and pass on the faith …
Lord Jesus, **grant your Spirit.**

For those who translate and distribute the Scriptures and all who read them …
Lord Jesus, **grant your Spirit.**

For those who bear witness to the love of Christ, through their speaking and caring, at home, at work, and in all situations of struggle or need …
Lord Jesus, **grant your Spirit.**

For all who, though mocked and persecuted for their faith, stand firm for Christ …
Lord Jesus, **grant your Spirit.**

For those who are beginning their journey as Christ's disciples …
Lord Jesus, **grant your Spirit.**

For those who doubt, or have lost their faith; and for those whose hearts are hardened and uncaring …
Lord Jesus, **grant your Spirit.**

We give thanks for those who have died in the faith of Christ …
Come then Lord and help your people, bought with the price of your own blood; and bring us with your saints to glory everlasting. Amen.

THE LORD'S PRAYER

(A HYMN may be sung)

CONCLUDING PRAYER

Lord Jesus Christ,
redeemer, friend and brother:
**may we know you more clearly,
love you more dearly,
and follow you more nearly,
day by day. Amen.**

(St Richard of Chichester)

(THE BLESSING or THE GRACE is said)

www.ingramcontent.com/pod-product-compliance
Lightning Source LLC
Chambersburg PA
CBHW070944080526
44587CB00015B/2212